ANOTHER DAY AFIELD

Also by the Lost Branch Sportsman's Club

Northwest of Someplace

ANOTHER DAY AFIELD

Hunting, fishing, and the places they lead us

Volume II

by
Greg Frey · Chris Smith · Jon Osborn · Jake Smith
THE LOST BRANCH SPORTSMAN'S CLUB

Copyright © 2022 by Greg Frey
Copyright © 2022 by Jon Osborn
Copyright © 2022 by Jake Smith
Copyright © 2022 by Chris Smith

All rights reserved. No part of this book may be reproduced, scanned, or distributed in any printed or electronic form or through any media or platform without written permission from the author of that story.

All artwork by Chris Smith and may not be reproduced without the artist's permission.

Some stories previously appeared in the following publications:

"Return to the Bog" by Greg Frey	*Michigan Out-of-Doors*
"Sunday Morning," by Greg Frey	*Gray's Sporting Journal*
"The Sentinel," by Jon Osborn	*Backcountry Journal*
"Help Wanted," by Greg Frey	*Gray's Sporting Journal*
"New Dog, Old Dog," by Chris Smith	*Ducks Unlimited*
"The Trapper's Cabin," by Chris Smith	*Ducks Unlimited*

"Stopping By Woods on a Snowy Evening" by Robert Frost is in public domain, as noted by Macmillan Publishers, 2/4/2021

Cover design by Brandon Hoffman

ISBN: 979-8-785-83880-2

Table of Contents

Foreword	1
Introduction	5
Return to the Bog	7
Anticipation	21
Fish Stories	25
And I Don't Even Deer Hunt	33
Sunday Morning	45
I Am a Fisherman	51
The Sentinel	57
Peace to All Who Enter	63
Help Wanted	73
New Dog, Old Dog	87
Common Scents	91
A Trifling of Flies	95
Walk With Me	105
The Trapper's Cabin	115
The Gift That Keeps on Giving	123
Backcountry	129

For our much *better halves...*

Kristin

Lani

Woods

&

Vickie

Thank you for joining us in this world.

Foreword

I've always been a Michigan fan. Part of that may be because of the rich fishing and hunting opportunities. Fly-rodders routinely find a lot of their streams and rivers listed in the top fisheries of the country. There's the Au Sable, the Pere Marquette, the Muskegon, and countless others like the Fox and the Manistee. Many opportunities exist for big spotted browns, spawning-colored brookies with red or orange bellies, lake-run steelies and salmon, and brawling smallies. When it comes to cutting loose a pointer or a setter, many folks head north and over the Mackinac Bridge. Isn't the Upper Peninsula on every grouse and woodcock hunter's bucket list? If I met a hard-core birddogger and he said it's not, I'd think again. We're stealthy, so I'd figure the odds are high that he probably wants to try to hog the coverts for himself. The same goes for duck hunters — there's no shortage of spectacular choices. Michigan's name, which comes from the Ojibwe word meaning "large lake," offers big-water hunting for divers, small marshes for puddle ducks, and rivers where you can float in a canoe for early season woodies and teal. Corker whitetail opportunities may not be the best, but volume makes up somewhat for of a lack of size.

If Michigan's sporting traditions are strong, then so, too, are the number of writers and artists. The state's rich, artistic legacy spans quite a wide range and makes it one of the epicenters for outstanding contributors to all facets of American words. We all know Ernest Hemingway, Jim Harrison, Steve Smith, and Thomas McGuane, as well as Joyce Carol Oats, John Voelker (aka Robert Traver), and Elmore Leonard. But there's also Ring Lardner, Nelson Algren, and Jay Nordlinger… along with hundreds more. They're great writers, playwrights, and poets, and they're all from Michigan.

While you're at it, you might as well add a few more names to that impressive list: Jake Smith, his brother Chris Smith, Jon Osborn, and Greg Frey are writers and artists of the first order. They have formed a hunting, fishing, and, I suppose by now, writer's group called the Lost Branch Sportsman's Club. If you're like my kids and don't notice bylines, that's okay, but I'd encourage you to take a closer look at some of the many sporting print and digital publications. You'll see their names or art in just about all of 'em, and it's not just now and again; it's virtually all the time.

When it comes to pursuits, some are social while others are solitary. Sailing and golf are best enjoyed with a cadre of similarly minded people. Running and swimming are solitary — it's difficult to chit-chat while gasping for air on a run, and it's hard to hear when underwater. Writing and sporting activities fall somewhere in-between. It's also best not to interrupt a writer at work just as it's a good idea not to chatter in a deer stand or while walking up on a grouse point. But after the fact, nothing beats camaraderie and the sharing of the experience. Life is about finding the balance between social and solitary, and that's what makes the Lost Branch Sportsman's Club so unique. Sometimes their lives are more solitary than that of a monk, while other times they come together to share and create. In many ways, they are the envy of us all.

Their first volume, *Northwest of Someplace*, showed a deep, emotional connection among family, friends, and the outdoors. Each story was written with the passion and understanding that can come from only those who drink from cups that runneth over. This, their second volume, *Another Day Afield*, picks up where *Northwest* left off. They write with conviction, texture, and a sensuality that makes us feel as if we're standing next to them. The voices contained in their sixteen chapters that are split equally are strong, mature, and developed. There is no waffling in their commitment to craft or to their devotion to lives best lived afield.

There may be another reason I'm fond of the state, and it's because it's known as the Mitten. If I don't know where a specific town is located, then natives simply hold up their hand and point. I do the same in my home of Cape Cod. Our island is shaped like a bodybuilder flexing his bicep. People laugh when I adopt my best pose and point, but that's probably because I need to hit the gym and grunt out a few more curls. The double barrel of Smiths are from above the pinky, while Frey lives near the tip of the ring finger and Osborn is below the knuckle of the pinky. Those coordinates are all near the woods, they're all near the marshes, and they're all near the water. And like all the other fine writers from Michigan, their reach extends beyond state lines. They stimulate our minds and touch our hearts, whether we're living next door or a thousand miles away.

It's quite simple to see what they see. All you have to do is sit in your favorite chair; ideally, you'll have a sleeping gun dog at your feet.

Then read. Their lyrical prose and sensual descriptions will do the rest. All of your troubles will be forgotten as you're immediately whisked away. Where you arrive will be a better place, one that will make you smile as you live through their experiences and relive your own.

—Tom Keer
Wellfleet, Massachusetts

Introduction

Putting together our first volume of hunting and fishing stories, *Northwest of Someplace*, felt like, for me, a walk through the bracken ferns on a quiet, dew-soaked October morning. A fog lingers about the thicket, no wind stirs, and the sun hasn't yet found its strength to burn off the chill. It's a place you've visited before so you know the way through, but the ferns hide the ground and somehow make the experience new again.

Then you see the short little spruce where your young setter went on point in her first season. You hear the stream where, halfway through the hunt, your Lab liked to impersonate a salmon so she could cool off. And the golden aspen leaves remind you of a sunset somewhere miles away and years ago when you sat on the gate of the station wagon with your dad and brother and ate candy bars and drank Coke from a glass bottle.

It was a trip of memories. Some of those stories were written many years ago, the experiences fresh in my mind – as I'm sure they were for Jon, Greg, and Chris – containing moments that thirty-some-odd-years had fogged over and hidden. I knew they were there, just like the familiar ground beneath the bracken, but they still felt new.

Joining together for our second volume was, to wear out an already worn-out phrase, "deja vu all over again." Certainly, new stories were written recalling more recent experiences, but mothballed ones emerged for freshening. Reading about those times, the younger times, and the vigor of hunting I did back then – particularly in the sportsman's paradise of South Dakota – I saw the promises I made myself of hunting and fishing all the time, damn whatever adult responsibilities lay on the horizon. Full game bags, stringers of fish, burnt gunpowder, muddy boots, exhausted dogs, go-go-go and never miss an opening day.

The truth is, those adult responsibilities that arrived on that horizon had other, glorious plans. That helping out with the marching band so you can watch your kids march or play percussion is an equally fulfilling way to spend a Saturday in October. Same as a cozy Sunday-morning fire before church when it really does look like a November duck day out the window but you decide it's okay to leave them unharassed. All those things that chipped away at the time able to be spent with shotgun or fly rod didn't cause resentment, like I suppose I assumed they would when I was younger. I found that they actually heightened the enjoyment of the outdoors and put so much more into perspective because they joined me on those times afield during the walks with good friends and dogs, or the chats with family around a campfire, or the quiet moments all alone just the river and me.

I suppose that's where the title of this book came from because in the end, that's all any of us can really hope for: Not limits or trophies or bucket-list items to cross off. Just another day afield.

—*Jake Smith*
Traverse City, Michigan

Return to the Bog

The day Grandpa dropped the bomb, he was sitting in his recliner, overalls on, staring at nothing. He did that often after Grandma died.

I was 17 and turning the corner on age and role reversal, which meant looking out for Grandpa instead of him looking out for me. Like a loyal dog, I lay on the carpet at his feet, thumbing through a magazine, hoping conversation would help take his mind off things. Deer hunting seemed a likely topic.

"So, where you going to sit on opening day?"

He shifted in his seat and paused, looking down as if noticing me for the first time.

"I don't think I'll go out this year."

My mind did a double take. Excuse me, what? I thought it was a logistics issue, physical mobility, as if he'd burden the rest of us.

"Well, you could sit with me. We could just sit together against the big oak tree along the creek bottom at the edge of the cornfield. It'll be fun. You can do the shooting. We'll walk down there together."

Grandpa smiled. "I just don't care if I ever shoot another deer."

I sat in numbed silence, trying to wrap my mind around this revelation. How could you not enjoy watching the sun come up over the hills and filter down through the dead, brown, rustling oak leaves in the branches overhead? How could your heart not race and your mind not explode with anticipation as you heard the crack of a branch breaking under the weight of something big, something distinctly different from the usual scurry of squirrels?

And for cryin' out loud, this was Shotgun Leo we're talking about. The man who in one season killed four deer with as many shots from his Remington slug gun. If legend has it right, three of them were on the run.

I puzzled over that conversation for years, not understanding it. I think I do now. And that thought, more than any, scares me.

Fast forward thirty-five years. Grandpa's gone. There's a pandemic. The summer river guiding season is over, and I teach forty sixth graders from home. Everything is new. Every lesson, every video tutorial, every Zoom meeting. Days go by creating Google Forms, Google Docs, Google Slides. I share screens and virtual whiteboards. Feedback must be instant and embedded. I work from seven a.m. until nine p.m. with maybe a couple hours off to eat dinner with the family and take the dogs for a walk. The fly shop calls for an occasional Saturday guide trip. I laugh at them. Without ten hours at the computer over the weekend, there are no lessons on Monday morning. I volunteered for this challenge because no one else would. The other thirty teachers in my building are apparently much smarter than I. But I'm becoming a grumpy old man in a hurry.

That's when the text came in from Drew. It was a Friday night, and my wife and I were standing in a long line at the high school football stadium. The line was made longer by the fact that we were six feet apart, and it was made slower by the fact that everyone who entered the stadium had to register their name. Furthermore, there was no football game. But at least we were fortunate to see our daughter's marching band show that narrowly escaped the cutting room floor of the pandemic. My phone buzzed, and I glanced at it, letting out a bemused snort.

My wife raised an eyebrow. "What is it?"

"Drew wants me to go duck hunting. Tomorrow morning." It was eight o'clock, dark already.

"You should go," Kristin insisted.

"I'd have to get a license, steel shot, I don't know where my decoys are, and, oh yeah — a Federal stamp from the post office." That was the deal breaker. No way that could happen overnight. (Ironically, all my virtual learning hadn't included buying a Federal stamp online, legally allowing you to hunt until the real one comes in the mail.) "Besides, I'm tired. I'd rather just sleep in and take a walk with you."

But after texting back a polite thanks and good luck, I felt bad. Drew had been reaching out all season like a puppy trying to get a cranky old dog to play. Our guide team is full of really nice, energetic young guys who have no greater purpose in life than to go fishing and drink beer. Not necessarily in that order. They live in a different world than me. But Drew is one of the kindest, and sometimes worlds collide, or at least overlap a little. Twenty years my junior, he belongs in a different era. Red-haired, good-humored, round boyish face, always smiling. He's the kind of guy who will correct you by saying, "You know, I think

I read… but I could be wrong," and you both know damn well that he's one-hundred-percent correct and it kind of pains him to tell you that you're full of crap. If he lived in the '50s, he'd definitely live in Pleasantville, and you'd describe him as a swell guy because he's… well, just a really swell guy. And here he was, doing his darndest to get me away from the computer, and once again I said no.

But there was an upside. Thoughts began stirring. I used to duck hunt. A lot. I had a boat with collapsible cattail walls, an outboard motor painted olive green, bags of decoys, the whole kit and caboodle. Hunting marshes near Michigan State University in homemade float tubes in college, I graduated to the Straits of Mackinac where big rollers came through under the bridge. Later, I stacked up flat chunks of limestone, hiding behind the rock walls as snow and ice and whistlers blew along the shores of Lake Huron. Paddling rivers for woodies, jumping teal from farm ponds, getting stranded on an island for sixteen hours — duck hunting was a passion, not a hobby. When I graduated high school, my counselor gave me a tie tack in the shape of a mallard that said, "Quack." That was over a span of about fifteen years, and that span ended twenty years ago. Now I bow hunt. And read books. Usually at the same time.

The change had been gradual. There was never a moment of outboard-engine-failure rage — fingers blistered from the starter cord, face hot and sweating, waves crawling over the transom of the boat. Nor an accident — no one almost shot off my cap or blew a hole in the boat. Places to hunt lost to development or competition didn't explain it. And I certainly never got so successful as to master the game and thereby destroy the fun in playing it. It was more like time slowly wore down enthusiasm like waves smoothing the rough edges of a boulder until my subconscious said, "This duck hunting thing is a lot of work. There must be better ways to have fun." And when that happened, something was lost. Something not recognized as missing until Drew brought it back.

A couple weeks went by. Amid the stress of this twenty-sixth year of teaching, I decided it was time to go back to camp in October. Marching band competitions, after-school robotics clubs, football games, college visits, family travels to downstate friends, and all the other activities that kept me from bowhunting at camp had ended this pandemic year. So other than staring at a computer screen six days a week, there was very little to do. That's when the dots connected. Take Drew to camp! Instead of hunting deer, hunt ducks. It was a win-win. Treat a friend to something he loved doing. Share with him the traditions of camp built over the years with my father and my longtime deer-hunting friend Todd. Todd would bow hunt, Drew and I would duck hunt, and Dad would help us get rid of all the good appetizers, food, and drink that we'd take to the cabin.

Suddenly the clouds cleared. My feet felt lighter. Trips to town became a joyful excuse to get away from the computer. I scoured the bare shelves of Dunham's for a box of Browning Waterfowl No. 4s, standing on tiptoes and blindly sweeping my arm across the darkest recesses of the top shelf.

For the first time ever, I cheerily stood in line at the Post Office. As I walked up to the counter, the lady asked how she could help.

"I'd like to buy a duck stamp." She frowned and leaned closer to the clear plastic shower curtain hanging as a divider over the counter. Thinking I hadn't spoken clearly through my mask, I turned up the volume.

"A duck stamp. I'd like to buy a duck stamp."

The frown wasn't going anywhere.

"Honey, we've got winter animals, trees, immaculate conception, stars and stripes… but no duck stamps."

Now it was my turn to be puzzled. "You mean you don't have any Federal duck stamps? They cost like twenty-five dollars?"

Then the light went on, and she actually laughed. I'm not sure if it was at herself or me. Probably me.

"Oh, you mean a Federal Waterfowl Stamp. Of course."

Of course. It never dawned on me that non-hunters might not associate duck and waterfowl as synonyms. Either way, it made the purchase of a duck stamp feel satisfying, like climbing Everest or solving a hard math problem. Carefully tucking the little piece of artwork in my wallet, I broke the rule of having to sign it and stick it on your license. If a warden asked, it'd be present, but desecrating such a fine painting of a duck seemed like a crime against waterfowl artists the world over.

Last but not least, a stop to the grocery to gather fried chicken, baked mac and cheese, sauerkraut, smoked sausage, giant soft pretzels, queso, German potato salad, and a case of retro-styled 1970s Old Milwaukee — all the fixings to recreate our church's Oktoberfest dinner, another covid casualty. Essentials acquired. Check.

The week before the road trip brought with it dismal rain and occasional sleet. I worked overtime every day, trying to make up for the work that would be missed on the weekend. On Friday late afternoon, Drew and I drove across the state in a steady rain and fog. But my spirits soared telling him about the camp and the social dynamics between my father, a devoted liberal, and Todd, a staunch conservative. The fact that the two can coexist peacefully (mostly) is a testament to the camaraderie of a deer camp and the fact that nature trumps Trump.

Pulling into the clearing near the big oaks and dark balsam firs, we saw smoke rising from the chimney. A rusted tin Stroh's sign near the cabin's door read "Welcome to the friendliest place in town." As we stepped into the cabin, I was greeted by the familiar sights of home away from home. A barrel stove squatted in the middle of the kitchen like a fat and happy pig. Dad and Todd were likewise sitting around a small table filled with meats and cheeses. They were leaning forward and arguing animatedly.

"But don't you think—" Todd interjected. It wasn't a question.

"You're on mute!" Dad held up the wand lighter to Todd's face, brandishing it like a sword, and clicked on the flame. A rather clever invention from two guys who hadn't spent more than five minutes on Zoom in the past six months. "Let me finish!"

Drew followed me into the bunk room so he could unpack his gear.

"You thought I was exaggerating."

Sometime during the night, the rain stopped. The following morning dawned fresh and crisp. We stepped out of the cabin into a night sky so clean that you could smell the towering balsams surrounding the cabin. A short drive down a two-track through a cedar swamp got us to the edge of the back-forty. Gathering up stools, a burlap gunny sack of decoys, and guns, we began our walk to the bog.

Dad had warned against following the old logging road to the bog. He and Mom had slogged down it to pick cranberries and struggled against the overgrowth, deep puddles, and muck. He had a much better route.

"Just go to the end of the shooting lane and head north through the cedars until you cut the road."

Problem was, he has a lot of shooting lanes, and they're all narrow and full of hummocks. They're also all very dark at five a.m. — not quite sure how far we'd bushwhack before cutting the trail again; it sounded like a sketchy plan. The logging road may have been overgrown and full of boot-sucking muck, but it was familiar — a devil I knew well.

We began our trek through the darkness of the swamp. Drew followed, a captive audience as I pointed out everything interesting that ever happened. We passed the stump where the bobcat stood, the trail the badger once walked, the tag alder thicket where my old blind used to lean before the clearcut took place, and the dark lane where the big ghost buck faced down Bret, the one he shot in the chest but never found. As we neared the tunnel of cedars entering the bog, I heard a commotion and looked back to see Drew missing. He had gone down, taken out by a natural anomaly: a foot-tall anthill hidden among cattails and switchgrass that reached our elbows. Why it was there, surrounded by ten inches of water, was one of life's mysteries, but not to the ants that live in it. Drew laughed it off, collected his gun and stool, and we plodded on.

When we passed an old metal Carlisle canoe stashed at the tree line, we stepped out onto the open bog. Stars were quickly dimming, a sure sign we needed to get our decoys in the water and hunker down. We splashed across the fifty yards of spiky, brittle cranberry bushes following twisting deer trails that made the walking slightly easier (as if walking through knee-deep water on shifting, moving, uneven ground while thorn-like branches clawed at your shins could ever be called easy). Carnivorous pitcher plants tempted insects with their cupped red and green leaves; they'd soon regret it as they slipped down a one-way tunnel into a cauldron of digestive liquid. Bouncing slightly, the cranberry bog's root mass floated atop a mixture of water and mud somewhere between the consistency of wet concrete and pancake batter. I'd been stuck in it, chest deep in waders, twenty years ago. It's a frightening experience.

After breaking out of the tree line and crossing seventy-five yards of bog, we came to the edge of the river, moving so slowly as to give the appearance of no current whatsoever. While canoeing it and throwing Johnson silver minnows into shallow pockets of reeds for hammer-handle pike during the summer, I had discovered that the riverbed itself is hard sand, covered by an inch or two of black muck. The middle of it holds knee-deep to waist-deep water. Quite safe, really.

The trick is getting there. As you near the edge, the bog itself curls and begins to sink into the bottomless black slurry. It's like floating on an air mattress that is slowly losing air on one side. You try to slide down on your bottom, but as you settle onto the bog, you're sitting in twelve to sixteen inches of water with nothing solid to hold onto other than brittle cranberry branches. Passing the point of no return, you slide off the bog and suck in your breath as the water rises toward the top of your waders. Simultaneously, your feet descend through the slurry, anxiously groping for hard bottom. By the time mine reached it, I was sporting two inches of freeboard and beads of sweat on my forehead.

Drew pushed the burlap sack of decoys toward the edge of the bog, the chosen half-dozen hand-picked for this morning's deception. A week ago, I had dragged them from the crawl space where they had slept for the last twenty years like castaways relegated to The Island of Misfit Toys. I started with Queenie, an ancient pintail washed up on the shore of Houghton Lake at my grandparents' cottage forty years ago. Why a decoy was named, and even more so named Queenie, is lost to time and the inner workings of a ten-year-old brain. The decoy was a connection with my grandparents, a portal to the summer day Queenie was found. A day of soft waves lapping the foam-laced shore, a maroon Johnson outboard and an aluminum rowboat filled with cane poles, bobbers, and bluegills in a big wire fish basket. Then came the Flambeau lightweight water-keel mallards, which were oxymoronically attached to one-pound steel brownies cut by my high school shop teacher thirty-five years ago. Drew politely pointed out that fact, and I had to agree it made no sense.

Ten minutes to legal shooting time. The sense of anticipation was palpable, like Christmas morning. I was giddy. There's no other word to describe it. When you're a 50-year-old curmudgeon, giddy feels good.

We settled onto our stools, Drew's taller than mine. His shoulders sat level with the cranberry bushes, and from a distance one had to look carefully to spot him. I had brought a low-riding turkey lounger and could immediately see that I could not. It was effective if one's goal was to stay completely hidden until birds were over the decoys. But if it was to watch the bog come alive and to enjoy the crimson and yellow maple hillside two miles distant, the turkey lounger was useless. Not to mention the fact my lap was underwater and my gun was kept dry by propping it across my knees. This would not do. How long should I suck it up and deal with it before caving to my OCD and heading back to the truck during prime shooting time to get a better chair? Ten minutes sounded about right.

Drew and I talked quietly yet excitedly, if such a thing can be done. Suddenly there was a loud *swoosh*, and four large mallards flew right over our decoys, twenty yards in front of us. They had come in low, hidden against the dark water and darker wall of tag alders on the far bank. Before we reacted, they were gone.

There was a moment of silence. Drew said, "We probably should have shot at those."

"I think so." We felt foolish, knowing at the same time it just didn't matter. Such is the state of grace when hunting with friends who get it.

Another ten minutes of silence. Frost glistened off the treetops as sunlight began to hit them. The early risers had left the marsh, and not a breath of wind stirred to bring ducks off Lake Huron, only a mile or two away.

A headache came on from straining to see above the cranberry bushes. "I'm going back to the truck to get a taller chair," I said.

Drew looked at me.

"I told you I had some issues."

Drew just shook his head. Grabbing my chair and gun, I was almost to the tree line when I heard two quick shots and turned to see a greenhead drop solidly from high in the sky. I gave Drew a thumbs up.

"I've got it," he hollered, then slipped hesitantly off the bog's edge as the water raced up to the top of his waders to greet him. Half an hour later, I returned with my other chair, sweating and exhausted but with a much better view of the marsh.

And the morning continued, as good as it had started. Every twenty to thirty minutes, we had ducks moving. Drew shot them. I missed them. Geese appeared downstream in a side-water slough. Unless you wanted to belly crawl through twelve inches of standing water in the cranberry bog, which amounted to swimming, not crawling, there was no way to touch them. They seemed to know that. They talked and splashed and spooked at our shots, leaving their honey hole briefly, returning ten minutes later to settle back in.

A bald eagle soared overhead, dropping low to inspect the decoys, flaring when it saw us. Four sandhill cranes appeared like distant bombers, miles off the horizon. Drew, on a retrieve to pick up a bluebill, crouched under the tag alders until they got close enough to realize they were not geese.

Mid-morning, chortling came from upriver. We hushed, thinking it might be divers swimming along the edge of the bog. The chortling and grunting grew more distinct. They were not ducks, causing a great deal of guessing. The mystery was solved as a family of three otters dove and frolicked, searching for small clams and crustaceans along the river bottom. Sunlight crept across the entire bog, turning red holly berries into sights of wonder against the grays and browns of the marsh.

Slowly, my giddiness turned flat as I realized this weekend would come to an end soon — much too soon. Drinking in the colors and smells of the bog, knowing I might not make it back again this season,

I tried to slow time, to somehow will it all to last a little bit longer. Soon all would be covered and silenced with winter's bitter white. It reminded me of Frederick, the little mouse in a children's book who ticked off his hard-working buddies by not gathering grains in the fall. He was actually gathering up all the colors and memories of summer to share with his fellow mice during the dark winter. Frederick had it right, even if he was a lazy slug.

All of this, all of the memories of this most extraordinary morning of waterfowling, is something I walked away from many years ago. Thanks to Drew, I'd regained a passion. Life can be funny that way. Sometimes it takes a pandemic and a change of normal living to come back to what really matters. I had walked the same road as Grandpa, and while I understood him, I had been offered a different path. One that I was glad I had taken.

—*Greg Frey*

Anticipation

Finally, a cool spell. Warmer-than-normal summer temps led to a more traditional August, pushing my annual "organize the hunting shed" day to the brink of September. To be sure, there were years when this most sacred of pre-season preparatory events occurred in haste as I untied last season's anchor-cord knots while swatting mosquitos the evening before a warm duck opener. But all things being equal, I savor this event for the first tease of autumn, when overnight lows dip to the mid-50s and low, gray clouds race overhead on a northwest wind.

As a younger lad, I wished August would last only long enough to enjoy a few precious hours on the beach and to fool a handful of late-summer trout, but it always seemed hunting season would never arrive. As marriage, jobs, and kids placed a premium on days afield, however, I pleaded with August to slow to a crawl, just as I do when October hits. This year didn't disappoint. Truth is, despite often intolerably hot weather, the last of the northerly summer months is worth savoring, like seeing presents under the tree for a month leading up to Christmas.

My gut says I'm maturing, realizing that, at almost 50, things eventually come to a close. As any "end" approaches — be it next week or another fifty years from now — so goes the stuff we crave, at least as far as earthly desires are concerned. My faith tells me there's a whole lot "better" waiting behind the veil, but while still subject to gravity on this big blue gem, I want to scrape every last bit out of the gallon of ice cream. For a sportsman, that means the various hunting and fishing seasons as they rear their annual heads.

And each season has its first day: Opening Day.

One thing about Opening Days is that despite the occasional one for the books, they disappoint more often than not concerning trigger pulls or hook-ups. Perhaps it's high expectations for a try at uneducated game or the memories from a solid season-ending hunt the previous year, but the opener strangely doesn't equal harvest like we hope, for a variety of reasons. The ten-point meticulously catalogued over the course of 500 trail-cam photos sleeps in; the couple-hundred geese using your neighbor's oat field trickle down to a mated pair; the red of a dozen steelhead becomes a haven for suckers; the brood of grouse in the Old Sofa Cover runs into an especially persistent goshawk. The point is, if *how many* dictates success, just shop at Walmart.

For those of us with a few layers of paint, the opener means just about everything *but* a stringer of limits, and tops on that list is the anticipation. It's walking out the door into a tangible chill drifting through the yard, indicating you'll need a fleece for the morning stroll with the dog. It's driving gravel county roads under the guise of a scouting mission for geese, knowing full well what you're really searching for: the first twinge of red and yellow on the roadside maples as the smell of fine pipe tobacco hints of past adventures. It's a chance to soak up a fall-like feeling without it actually being here, for when it does begin, it'll all be over too quickly, and, as Gene Hill so perfectly stated, "...another year must pass before we can walk this way again."

But more than even the cool morning walks or color tours cloaked as scouting trips, my favorite way to anticipate is sorting and replacing gear — which has become a sport in itself — in the "Duck Shed."

Never one to be accused, or even suspected, of being orderly, I throw off any such scent with a hunting shed that to all but the specially trained would appear, shall we say... messy. The Good Wife uses more colorful words. From the first of September through the end of December, though, it's really not too bad. And I have company. The decoys and deer stands share rent space with a handful of mice who help keep things tidy by repurposing plucked duck and goose feathers for their beds. A few wasps occupy a nest under the outside eaves, safe from harm as long as they honor our truce.

A specialist who hunts one bird with minimal methods would get by with a corner of a garage or the leftover space under the stairs by a water softener or hot-water heater. But not the fella who tries to do it all. Early goose season morphs into the onset of ducks and geese, coinciding with the whitetail bow opener and salmon run, woodcock and grouse, fall steelhead, then the waterfowl migration needing large decoy setups and layout boats. Right on its heels rides the high-powered rifles of deer camp, followed by more steelhead, punching doe tags before Christmas, and maybe even a New Year's grouse to cap things off in style. Oh, and throw in an old-fashioned squirrel hunt whenever the mood strikes. How could *anyone* keep all that straight without being organized?

This urge to obtain and maintain gear fuels my anticipation of coming seasons more than anything. When that right weather hits, I pour a glass of whatever remains, light a cigar, and head to the shed. Since our waterfowl season typically ends in a fury of numb fingers and two feet of snow, gear isn't stowed as gracefully as it should be; it's tossed in as early winter makes a vicious grab at any unprepared soul. Shutting the door — sometimes kicking in a stray decoy with an icy boot — I grin, and not just because of the much-needed, hearthside thaw that awaits. When next August arrives, and the first cool northwest winds swish green leaves against the house, I'll get to untangle everything and start the anticipation all over.

—*Chris Smith*

Fish Stories

The trout's shadow flickered across the cobbled bottom. Even viewed from above, the shimmering silhouette was barely discernable — more innuendo than actual fish. Those ruby spots and buttery flanks, so vibrant above water, blended perfectly with the sand, pebbles, and submerged wood.

The angler crouched on a bluff overlooking the creek. His sweat-stained hat faded among the ferns and fallen trees, and a battered fiberglass spinning rod rested within easy reach.

Rumors had led him there — hardware-store gossip, to be exact. At first, he'd gone simply to buy nuts and bolts, but eventually his emphasis shifted. Then he began loitering in the isles — list in hand, pretending to shop — listening to the old-timers swap tales of legendary trout and secret streams.

Most of them had graduated into armchair anglers by then, but they still adored trading lies about fish caught and lost, different types of tackle, and which waters fished best. Their discussions often centered around tiny local brooks bearing names like Mann, Silver, and Gun. But there was one other worth mentioning: Bear Creek. Whenever *that* name came up, the conversation assumed a hushed, reverent tone.

Finally, he'd had enough, so one morning, the man drove south on M-40, turning onto a gravel two-track near a small cemetery. Nosing the rusty Nova into the woods, he idled along until hemlock boughs brushed the fenders, forcing him to park.

Hiking down to the water, he paused at likely looking holes, plumbing the depths with nightcrawlers, and catching steelhead smolts by the dozen. But naïve riffle rainbows weren't the focus, so he pressed deeper into the woods. Around noon, he stopped on a steep, sandy bluff overlooking the creek, where the high sun and elevated perspective offered a portal into the underwater world below.

That's when he saw it — a brown trout with reddish fins, dime-sized spots, and a curved, kype jaw. For a while he simply stared, ignoring the whining mosquitoes, resisting a niggling temptation to lob a hasty cast. Such a trophy demanded patience, and a plan.

Minutes passed while he plotted his approach, calculating the particulars of drift and delivery. As the sun angled across the sky, however, the light changed, and the fish faded away. He panicked, and doubt crept in, filling the void where the trout once swam. Had the vision been some figment of his imagination? Some hydrologic trick perhaps? Cursing his luck, he squinted hard, scanning the riffle again and again, trying to will the trout into existence.

He simmered in his frustration, but the light gradually shifted, and the sleek, torpedo-shaped profile reemerged alongside a sunken log. The trout never had left, of course, but now he could see it, plain as ever. Breathing a sigh of relief, the man opened his bait box, plucked out a nightcrawler, and threaded it onto an Aberdeen hook.

One shot, that's all he'd get. The bait must drift naturally, unencumbered by split-shot or drag. With a little luck, the trout would inhale the offering on the first pass — that or evaporate into obscurity. It was that simple. He inched forward, worming along the ridge on his elbows, sweat streaming down his neck. *Why did catching this fish matter so much?* He couldn't find the words, but he felt the importance at his core.

The bail flipped with a muted click, and the crawler dropped into the current.

Plop.

The bait splatted softly into the corrugated riffle, a dozen or more feet below the ledge. Following its progress with his rod tip, the man held his breath.

One cast. One chance. *Just that simple.*

Something flashed white, down there in the gloom. The worm vanished, the line drew taught, and the rod bent into a deep arc. As the trout thrashed the water to a froth, the man quickly realized the limitations of his bargain-basement tackle. Uncertainty flooded his mind, and he began fretting over the knot, his decision to use last-season's line, and the questionable strength of that old Eagle Claw hook.

So many variables... so much at stake.

He rushed downhill, tumbling ahead of an avalanche of sand and sticks... imagining the popping recoil of the line snapping, of the trout swimming free. He pictured a deflated version of himself telling the story of the big one that got away — that tired old fish story no one ever believes. Splashing bearlike into the stream, he pinned the trout to the bottom, and with a hooked index finger, he hefted his dripping prize aloft....

· · · · · · · · ·

I was barely out of diapers when I first heard the story of The Bear Creek Brown. My dad was the worm-lobbing protagonist, and his words painted a vivid image of what transpired that day. I could see every spot on that trout... hear the swarms of mosquitoes... see the nightcrawler tumbling downstream toward the fish. Even then, I could *feel* his excitement and understood why that trout meant so much.

To this day, I carry that narrative around like some kind of piscatorial treasure map — a compass heading that hopefully leads to my own version of Dad's fish. One thing's for sure: Forty years later, and a father myself, fishing still consumes my thoughts, distracts me constantly, and keeps me awake at night. To make matters worse, when I finally *do* nod off, trout dominate my dreams. Not bratwurst-sized fish, either; the salmonids of my subconscious are broad-shouldered browns wearing red and black spots, hoodlums that lurk beneath logjams by day, accosting mayflies, mice, and wayward amphibians by night.

That a forty-year-old fish story could prompt this obsession amounts to madness. Trout Madness, Traver would have called it.

Flash forward, now, to my own middle age. The same sickness that afflicted my father led me to Sand Creek. Like him, I found my home water by following rumors, by pursuing wild tales of froggy flats, emerging mayflies, and oversized, unpressured trout.

The upper reaches of this creek run gin-clear and cold, with a clean, sandy substrate; but farther downstream, the current drifts slowly past silt-laden banks. All trout streams have unique personalities, and this one is dismal and dour, as nearly all the best brown trout water is. My companions and I refer to these sluggish streams as "Murder Water," half-expecting to find the local gas station attendant floating face down in an eddy. Funny when confronting the night together, but macabre humor assumes another meaning when fishing alone.

But it's not dark yet, and the humid air swells with possibilities. Casting foreboding thoughts aside, I idle the pickup down a gravel two-track, parking where a wall of tag alders borders the banks. A storm is brewing in the distance, and the air smells of ozone. Heat lightning flickers like distant artillery, and thunderheads mass like advancing troops, their rumbling cannonade growing louder as they approach.

Hiking a mile or more along the water, I survey likely looking holes and current seams. So far, I've seen no evidence of risers, hatches, or spinner falls, so I plop down on the bank to formulate a plan. Just then, a subtle bulge betrays a feeding fish. Nothing splashy — the big ones seldom are — just the confident cadence of an undisturbed trout. The leopard spotted hump barely breaks the surface tension as it porpoises lazily, just beneath the surface.

For a while, I simply watch, ignoring the mosquitos humming around my ears, resisting the temptation to cast some random fly in haste. Experience makes large trout particular, wise — even downright suspicious, not unlike old men. They're less wary in the gloaming, but fooling this fish will require patience, and a plan.

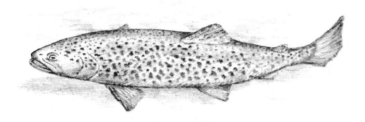

The river flows slick as motor oil — no riffles to conceal casting imperfections; no place for slopping down a leader or slurping a fly off the surface to recast. I peruse the battered old Wheatly box. It's mid-June. The drakes are winding down, leaving mahoganies and maybe the beginnings of a Hex hatch, but there's no indications of that yet. Overhead, swooping waxwings intercept an occasional caddis, but that's the extent of the insect activity.

An Iso spinner seems as good a choice as any. It's a Goldilocks fly — not too big, not too small... just right. It's big enough to get noticed but without the splatter associated with a larger Hex dun. Creeping along the bank, I step softly to avoid the telltale vibrations that always send trout scrambling for cover.

Three rod lengths away from where the rings last appeared, I begin casting. The delivery and drift look perfect to my imperfect eye, but the trout, assuming it's still there, shows no interest. Again and again the *Isonychia* imitation settles upon the water, each time intentionally left or right of where it floated previously. A dozen passes later, however, there's still no sign of the fish.

Times like these call for a pipe and more observation. Scratching a match to life, I cup my hand around the bowl, but a breeze puffs out the flame. The Blue Tip hisses as it lands in the water, spinning lazy circles in the current. That's when I notice something floating in the film: spinners. But not the maroon-hued mayfly on my leader. *Ephoron leukon*, white flies.

Almost on cue, the trout rises again, although slightly upstream this time. Maybe it's not even the same fish, but the casual feeding rhythm appears similar. Rifling through the fly box with renewed vigor, I pluck out a Light Cahill that hasn't seen service in a dozen years. Daylight's fading fast. It's not so dark that I need the headlamp yet but dim enough to challenge my aging eyes. Feeding fish always frustrate the knot-tying process, but in the end, a steady tug on the leader proves it strong. The Cahill settles into the bubble line, just upstream from where the rings dissipated only moments before.

For a few seconds, the fly loiters but then suddenly vanishes. No splash, no bulging roll. Simply gone. Raising the rod, the stout bamboo bows into the cork, a heavy fish pulsing on the opposite end. I'm optimistic as I immediately recoup some line, but upon feeling resistance, the fish dashes downstream, and I realize I'm clearly outgunned, despite all the fancy tackle.

The following few minutes are a tense game of cat-and-mouse, with the trout seeking safety in log jams, and me taxing the leader, rod, and reel to their utmost capacity. I nearly net the fish twice, but each time it surges away, dangerously close to breaking off. I manage to get a close look though, near enough to see the thumb-sized black and red spots, buttery-yellow flanks, and sneering kype jaw. I desperately want to land this fish, to cradle it, to call it my own — if even for a moment.

With the backing beyond the rod tip now and the trout far downstream, slack builds in the line. A fish this large could always straighten the hook, not to mention the fact that that protracted battles wear ever-widening openings in the fleshy area where the hook penetrates the jaw. The more time that passes means more opportunity to escape.

So many variables... so much at stake.

Leveraging the rod sideways, I apply maximum pressure, and the bamboo creaks under the load. It feels like the tide might turn. It does, but not in my favor. With a final head shake, the line goes inexplicably limp.

In the aftermath, I realize *not* catching that trout ensures it will always endure larger than life — a legend that remains immeasurable, enigmatic... almost immortal. After all, nothing dilutes legend like cold hard facts. Mystery, paradox, longevity. These are what make fish stories so endearing — and the reason they've resounded in caves, around campfires, and throughout small-town hardware stores ever since that first big one slipped away.

Returning from the river after dark, I close the cottage doors quietly so as not to wake the kids. They're sleeping, probably dreaming about sports, music, or movies. Somehow, they missed the Trout Madness gene and don't obsess over rods, reels, and flies like their old man. Maybe life's easier that way. Either way, come morning, they're sure to ask, "Dad, did you catch anything last night?"

"Have a seat," I'll tell them, topping off my coffee. "Let me tell you a fish story."

—*Jon Osborn*

And I Don't Even Deer Hunt

Unlike the other members of the Lost Branch Sportsman's Club, I don't deer hunt. Chris views quiet time in a tree stand — which may or may not involve simply straddling a sturdy limb — as nothing more than a worthy alternative to working when there's a lull in the duck season. Jon walks the edge of marital discord to sneak out for a couple of hours on opening day hoping for one lucky shot after spending all of October chasing grouse, woodcock, and ducks. Greg, on the other hand, is dyed-in-his-Mackinaw-wool jacket. Buffalo plaid, Stormy Kromer, the whole deal. A thick knife on his hip and a favorable wind simmers his blood.

"Deer Camp" in Michigan is a heritage connecting generations and spawning absurd songs that, if you listen closely, contain several kernels of truth. Carrying on the rich tradition of Michigan whitetail hunting in our family falls upon my wife's shoulders on her parents' 200 acres of farmland, swamp, and forest. I've sat in the blind with Vickie and watched through binoculars as she dropped a spike right where it stood; and my mouth fell when she stopped a cantering, crippled deer we inadvertently pushed too soon, snaking a .44 round through the aspens better than any ruffed grouse shot. Joining both of her parents in deer blinds her entire life, Vickie was eager to wrap our three kids into the fold, placing a rifle in their hands and whispering in their ears to hold steady and squeeze. Each child has shared those individual, treasured moments in the deer blind with their mother — moments I wouldn't dream of intruding upon, when it becomes something so much more than deer hunting.

My deer season consists of food. "Farm-to-table" may be a term coined by properly manicured and falsely attired devotees of the weekend farmer's market downtown, but this connection to the land is far older and purer for those who get dirt under their fingernails. So while I putter away at meals back at the in-law's farmhouse — waiting on the gang to return to warm up and fuel up and then joining in the tracking — I also enjoy the butchering, grinding, packaging, cooking, and eating. These medallion loin steaks will be excellent seared in cast iron and finished in a bourbon-and-red-wine sauce; this summer will be the year of homemade smoked brats; three packages of cubed roast for those dead-of-winter stews; there's a new grinder attachment for sausage snack sticks I'm itching to try; and by all means, the more burger the better for spaghetti sauce, meatloaf, chili, tacos, shepherd's pie, and bacon-cheeseburger sliders for the Super Bowl.

The gutting, however, goes to whomever pulled the trigger.

My daughter Maddie and I sat in the farmhouse deciding what to make the hungry hunters for dinner when the phone chirped. Our older son, Pete, 14 at the time, hit a big buck, but it ran off. He and Vickie were waiting and would let us know. I'd experienced this lather-rinse-repeat process dozens of times during deer seasons past on the Schafer farm; so Maddie and I changed into our "hunting" clothes to await word of assistance for tracking, hauling, and hanging.

"Why haven't they called yet?" Maddie asked after nearly an hour.

Surely they found something by now, I thought. A text went out to the group. No luck.

In the meantime, my other son, Mark, returned deerless with John, my father-in-law. After a conversation between him and mother-in-law Kathy, they made the "all-hands-on-deck" call.

A few miles from their farm and 120 acres sits their other eighty acres, a wooded wonderland. Some of my earliest pre-kid memories of weekend excursions with Vickie to the cabin involve raising tower deer blinds, felling trees and splitting wood, waging a war of attrition against a pesky beaver that liked to clog up the culvert under the trail along their cozy pond, and hoping to stumble upon a grouse or woodcock. Deer season in the old cabin — since demolished for their permanent retirement residence at the farmhouse — was a magical time, even for this non-deer hunter. I loved watching the gang head off into the darkness, their blaze orange glowing softly in dim flashlights, and I'd leave a window cracked to listen for a rifle shot, ready to burst out of the cabin into the chilly November air to help track. A prized bird-hunting memory occurred steps from the cabin when our old setter Allie skidded to a halt on the trail and pointed — a rare occurrence — and a fat grouse flushed, banking high over the trail. In an even rarer occurrence, I snapped off a shot with my 16-gauge Fox, and the bird cartwheeled. Behind me stood six-year-old Pete, his mouth hanging open and his eyes wide at the shocking taste of this wonderful wild world. Since a torn cruciate ligament sidelined our Lab Josie, I sent him in for the retrieve among the autumn olive thorns. Pete still has the empty shell somewhere, and the photo of him and me and a wet Allie and grouse is one of the few photos he took with him to college.

On the property's back boundary, we convened at the deer blind where Pete took his shot: Vickie, Pete, Mark, Maddie, John, Kathy, and me.

"Which deer is it?" Kathy asked.

"It's big, but I think it's just a spike," Vickie replied. "Strange antlers. Long."

At the mention of antlers, my eyes widened.

"Ah... *that* one," Kathy said. "We've seen him on the trail camera. I'm glad Pete shot. Frankly, we don't want that deer breeding."

"He made a good shot," Vickie said, "but it's a big deer. It might go a ways. We found a little blood trail heading toward the neighbor's property."

With mutual agreement to track deer on each other's property, searching there didn't bring the sigh and slouch from John and Kathy. Rather, it was where Vickie pointed — toward a pond and its surrounding swampy bog.

Pete looked worried.

"It probably hit the edge of the pond and stopped," Vickie told him. "There's nowhere else for it to go. Everything will be fine. I bet we'll find it right on the edge."

Fanning out, we pushed through the woods, discovering more blood and buoying our hopes. The maples and birches and aspens gave way to squatty alders and willows, the ground sloping and growing squishy underfoot. Soon, marsh grasses pulled at our ankles. Through the trees, I spotted a thin line of water — the pond.

Up ahead, Kathy called, "Found it." She didn't sound excited.

I made my way to Kathy and Pete, spotting my son's disconcerted grin through the alders. Vickie had been right: The deer — an absolute monster of an animal — ran to the pond's edge and stopped. Apparently, crashing through the hummocks of vegetation and lunging into the deep channels dissecting the perimeter bog sapped the last of the deer's strength. One final surge couldn't clear the next bit of vegetation, and there it lay, its snout and one long antler exposed above the water's surface, trapped in the bog, dead.

"We have good news and bad news," I told my wife when she made it to the shore, standing on wobbly hummocks of leatherleaf. She saw both for herself.

"How stuck is it?" she asked.

I reached for the obnoxiously long single antler jutting skyward and gave a little shake.

Apparently, the deer wasn't that stuck.

Nor that dead.

In a giant geyser, Pete's deer leapt to the sky, over the last ridge of vegetation, and began swimming. A hundred yards away, in the center of the pond, it slowed, succumbed, and circled in its final throes.

I laughed. The kind of laughter when something really isn't funny but you don't know what else to do and you don't want to curse in front of your in-laws and kids so you just sort of laugh.

"Well this is new," Vickie muttered.

Pete panicked. I'm sure he pictured himself standing there, helpless, watching his hulking buck sink and vanish right before his eyes.

Like I said, I don't deer hunt. But I am a dad. And I've lost crippled birds before, each one leaving a pit in my stomach. I imagined that feeling exponentially worse for a deer — especially in a boy's young hunting career — and resolved not to let my son go through that.

"Hey, what do I always tell you?" I put my arm around Pete's shoulders. "There's always a solution." I reminded him of the miniscule makeshift wheel strut of an F-16 model airplane I carved out of a spare bit of plastic to replace the factory part devoured by his bedroom carpet. "The solution may not be easy, but there's always one."

Debate over the whereabouts of John and Kathy's small boat — and its sea worthiness — made a solution seem a bit murky at best for the moment, however. Kathy, Mark, and Maddie headed back to the cabin for the ATV and to evaluate the boat — if they even found it.

"It's a nice day," I said to Vickie, gazing up at the brilliant blue sky. A rare Indian-summer day in November: dry, warm, and making me wish it were still grouse season. "I'll just strip down and swim out there."

If you are blessed with a significant other in your life, you've no doubt uttered a phrase or two in your time together that's led this spectacular angel to give you the "look." Head tilted, lips drawn straight, eyes filled with an internal despair at the workings of the universe that made her foolishly believe the man she's staring at right now was the best she could do.

"At least wear a life preserver," she muttered before catching up to her mom. Maybe she hoped the swim would wash away the stupidity. Frankly, I think she just wanted to avoid all the life insurance paperwork.

We kept an eye on the deer — a few inches of antler tip visible. I wasn't too keen about swimming — although a beautiful day, it was still November — but unless they found the boat, I didn't see how else the animal would make it to shore. And the way the conversation went between John and Kathy, that life preserver seemed like not just the best solution but the only one.

Some solutions come unexpectedly, though.

"Is that deer getting closer?" I asked Pete. His younger eyes squinted. He agreed.

Soft ripples on the surface indicated a breath of a breeze. Blowing toward us.

Seems God had a solution, too. Probably His laughter blowing the deer to shore.

By the time the troop returned with a life preserver and a rope — and no boat — the dead deer drifted to fifteen yards from shore. So close, and yet a swim still appeared inevitable.

After securing the rope to a hefty, dead tree branch, we took turns heaving it at the deer, hoping to snag the single antler. It's hard to throw a limb when you're balancing precariously on a bog hummock, working into a breeze, muscles aching from disbelieving laughter. Eventually, someone — I think John — plopped the branch barely on the other side of the antler. The crowd cheered. Delicate pulling brought the animal closer until, locked in a human chain leaning dangerously over the water, John grabbed the antler and yanked the deer the last several feet to shore. Cue the applause and backslaps.

But I noticed John eyeing the deer carefully. We tried hauling the water-logged monster up onto the hummock, and our spent muscles couldn't budge it. The congratulations turned once more to bewilderment. Being now within our grasp — quite literally — didn't appear to get us much closer to getting this thing back onto dry land.

After reefing, struggling, and otherwise willing a burst of heretofore unrealized superhero powers into existence, we managed to raise its head up out of the slop enough to secure a rope around it. Lashing the other end to the ATV back up on dry ground, we pulled and pushed while the four-wheeler assisted, and succeeded in dragging the deer up over the first hummock before it crashed through the bog again. I considered simply erecting a headstone and calling it good.

"This isn't going to be fun," John said. Apparently, our motto for the day.

He dropped to his knees, the bog water in front of him, and proceeded to rid the deer of a significant amount of weight by gutting it into the pond while Pete and I each held a splayed leg. Considerably lighter — and driven by adrenaline-fueled exasperation — we bounced across several more hummocks and dragged Pete's buck into the alders and eventually the dry aspens. With one final heave, we deposited it onto the ATV's trailer.

"We've got a few hours of daylight left," Vickie told Mark. They scampered to a vehicle to finish out opening day in a blind at the farm, and I hitched a ride back to the cabin on the ATV.

John prepared the pulley in the garage where Pete's deer would hang until butchering the next day. But first we needed to hoist it into a tree and give the cavity a good rinse, washing out blood to minimize the dripping onto the garage floor. Usually, it takes only a person or two to pull the rope over the thick oak branch, but even with a pulley's help, we barely raised the massive deer's front end off the ground.

"Let's tie it to the ATV," Kathy suggested. "I'll push the deer up while someone drives and pulls."

Pete — feeling like he hadn't done much other than make a tough shot that led to everyone else's suffering, a silly notion, we assured him — volunteered. But, being 14, his spindly weight and the engine's horsepower weren't enough. He needed more ballast, so I hopped onto the back of the ATV, and, like a bag of cement adding weight to the back of a pick-up truck for traction, knelt down and held on and told Pete to ease it forward.

Twenty years earlier, on a dirt road off the coast of Lake Superior, my brother Chris and I set out on a sunny Sunday in April. The road led to the Coast Guard's remote — and abandoned — Vermilion Life Saving Station, a place where Lake Superior State University's ornithology class regularly banded all manner of hawks, falcons, and songbirds. Somewhere almost directly offshore, in the tumult of the greatest of the Great Lakes, lay the *Edmund Fitzgerald*, and I had oftened wondered if the Vermilion Station heard Captain McSorley's final transmission that the boat and crew were holding their own.

Chris and I had wanted to explore Vermillion and see if we could make it back there and spot some birds. April in the Upper Peninsula sees incredible snow drifts lingering in the forests' shady spots, yet the sun is warm enough to melt where it reaches the ground. The sun-dappled trail to Vermillion stretched before us into the wilderness, sloppy as a pig farm.

Chris revved the two-wheel-drive S-10 pickup. "We got this."

"Um…" I tried to reply. But I'm the little brother.

We made it maybe a hundred yards before discovering the next couple of miles lay in shadow and, therefore, a snowdrift up to our navel. A sixteen-point turn later, we aimed back the way we came.

The mud won after about ten feet.

"I've got cement in the back, but we need more weight," Chris said.

I rolled down my window to search for stumps, branches, rocks, anything in the surrounding forest. Chris's stillness and silence hung like a shapeless menace, a thing alive. He stared at me.

The little brother.

He jabbed his thumb to the open truck bed.

While Chris yee-hawed like a rodeo cowboy strapped to a fiendish bull named Widow Maker or something else equally alarming, he kept the gas floored, the truck fishtailing down the trail and through the mud. Except Chris wasn't the cowboy. I was. And as we slammed into rut after rut, there reached a point when, hovering in mid-air and completely detached from the truck and Earth itself, I glanced over to see forty pounds of solid cement eye-level.

We made it back to civilization, and, surprisingly, I didn't die. Something we marveled at time and again during our college days at LSSU.

That experience of flying came back to me not so much as a wistful, crazy college recollection but an actual moment to relive as I soared into that brilliant blue November sky when Pete accidentally jammed the throttle. For one solitary moment, I felt like a bird.

But humans don't fly. They crash to the ground. Hard. And after a complete revolution, that's precisely what I did.

I wasn't the only one unable to momentarily breathe. There stood

Kathy — my wonderful, sweet, compassionate mother-in-law — hands on her knees, doubled over, wheezing.

Pete, on the other hand, appeared as if he'd just poked the eyes of Satan. He rushed to my side and helped me sit up, and after he saw his teenage years wouldn't be spent in a single-parent household, he started to laugh, too.

Like I said: And I don't even deer hunt.

The deer finally secured to the tree, Kathy informed me that, since the cabin now sat uninhabited, the water had been shut off. We needed to drive back to the farm and fill up a few five-gallon buckets with water to rinse out the deer. I volunteered. My good friend Tylenol sat at the farm.

I wanted the day to be over. *Needed* the day to be over. Every bone ached, and I wasn't entirely sure I hadn't fractured or torn something in my knee. Returning to the cabin and hobbling from the back of our SUV, the heavy buckets of water pulling at my weak and useless arms, I convinced myself that enough strength remained to generate some swinging momentum with the buckets to douse the inside of the deer.

At one point, earlier in the day, watching the results of God's laughter blow the deer back to shore, I thought I witnessed an honest-to-goodness miracle in avoiding the need to take a dip in the pond and being able to stay dry.

The words, "Uh-oh," might have escaped my lips when I let the water from the bucket fly. In one collective wave, it sloshed inside the cavity and careened right back out to where it came from.

For the record, bloody deer gut water tastes about like you'd expect.

    . . . .

The clerk at the country convenience store raised an eyebrow when I walked in — drenched, limping, muddy. I still had dinner to make. Earlier in the day, Maddie suggested tacos. Perfect. Brown some venison burger, set all the fixings on the table, and let everyone make what they wanted. I could do this.

Hobbling up and down the three aisles, I finally spotted the taco shells and sauce. On the bottom shelf. Of course. I must've sounded like a 90-year-old man when I knelt on the only partially crippled knee — one hand on my back, the other on the shelf for support and to prevent a face-plant in the aisle — and I felt no shame at the thought that asking the clerk for help in standing seemed a distinct possibility.

My wallet never felt so far out of reach sitting there in my back pocket.

Now, when I'm at the farm and the phone warbles with a text from an excited deer hunter, my hand hesitates in answering it. And my eye twitches. After all, I don't even deer hunt.

—Jake Smith

Sunday Morning

Sunday morning, November. We are trudging through the swamp before daylight. I'm leading. This is my camp, my swamp, our hunt. I use the flashlight sparingly because it makes things leap out at you, and you're better off feeling your way in the dark. After all, as they say, it's rarely "pitch dark" in the woods. Mostly you can see twigs and logs and a somewhat distinct path.

Bret follows, his long legs slowed by my groping pace. We've been hunting partners for more than seven years now, which to anyone who hunts is a much stronger bond than simply being friends. Hunting friendships require so much more by way of patience, mutual respect for the game one pursues, and willingness to face predicaments together. We've been stranded on Sulphur Island, stuck to our waists in muck at Devils Lake, and climbed to the top of the world in Colorado's Medicine Bow mountains. All this since I took his sister to the senior prom. Romance's loss was hunting's gain, and in hindsight, I guess, I wouldn't trade the relationships.

For hunters, Sundays are melancholy days, unless you're on some sort of extended vacation. You're hunting, but you also know that by noon you better think about packing up and the long drive back to the city where you make the money that makes all this possible.

So as we stumble back through the swamp in the dark, I already feel tired and cross. We settle along an old logging trail in a dense stand of cedars. Bret faces east and I face west, a damp cedar between our backs. We sit in silence, waiting for the distinct snap that will signal a deer moving cautiously through the swamp.

The darkness turns to gray, and within about twenty minutes, the imperceptible change between night and day occurs, though the swamp always favors darkness. Another half-hour passes, and I'm beginning to lose interest when I hear Bret whisper:

Whose woods these are I think I know.
His house is in the village, though;
He will not see me stopping here
To watch his woods fill up with snow.

My little horse must think it queer
To stop without a farmhouse near
Between the woods and frozen lake
The darkest evening of the year.

He gives his harness bells a shake
To ask if there is some mistake.
The only other sound's the sweep
Of easy wind and downy flake.

The woods are lovely, dark, and deep,
But I have promises to keep,
And miles to go before I sleep,
And miles to go before I sleep.

I ponder the poem in silence and then am reminded of a discussion with a literary friend.

"That poem's about suicide," I whisper.

"What?"

"The poem — it's about suicide," I repeat.

Bret's quickly defensive, hesitant to have me ruin his favorite poem with a dark analysis. I can almost hear him mouthing the word, looking for some hidden meaning that eluded him before.

"How in the hell do you get suicide out of *that?*" he finally replies.

"No, seriously," I whisper. I'm looking at the dark cedars around me. Still no movement. Even the jays are silent, and I wonder if I can quite explain it, knowing full well the answer. Nevertheless, it is Sunday morning, and the closest whitetail is on the downtown buck pole at the Credit Union.

"The guy is sitting in the middle of the woods in the snow wondering whether to plug himself or not when he starts thinking about his family and everyone back home. It's about suicide," I explain.

"You can't logically say that poem is about suicide unless you read into it," Bret whispers.

I have to wonder if maybe he's not right. But then I wonder if he isn't just living on the surface because it's easier there. Still, the woods are quiet and calm and empty. It looks as though another season is going to pass without so much as a glimpse of a buck.

"Bret, think about that line 'The darkest evening of the year.' Tell me there's no meaning behind that. Tell me he just happened to stop in those woods the night of the winter solstice," I whisper.

I can tell Bret is getting into the argument. He leans his rifle against the tree and carefully places his gloved hands by his hips so he can shift his weight in silence. He cranes his neck. I can see the steam from his breath when he whispers.

"*That's exactly* what I'm trying to tell you."

And just for a moment, I want to believe it, too. I want to believe Frost meant nothing more than that, but it is not to be. The mood of this place, as in so many others I've hunted, doesn't promote this optimism. It makes me feel dark, cold, and wet. The magazines and coffee-table books never make it look that way. The hunter is usually posed on some vista with a mule-deer buck's rack neatly lashed to his pack frame. From that vantage, one might be led to believe in surface niceties, but deer hunting in Michigan is cold and gray. A few years ago, my cousin came in at noon on opening day and didn't hunt the rest of the season. It was the first he had missed in 10 years. A month before, his wife had left him, and he later confided it wasn't a good idea to be alone in a November woods with gun in hand. There's nothing lovely about a stark woods in November.

I stare into the cedars, refusing eye contact with Bret. They say there are hills you will die on, and I prepare to make my last stand. A flock of mallards buzzes the gray skyline above the cedars.

"C'mon, Bret! Think about it: 'The woods are lovely, dark, and deep.' It's all a metaphor for his feelings. He's alone. He's depressed. How can you *not* see it?" I whisper.

"Greg, the poem is about life and how it can be long and hard. Frost is saying we're never really home. Nothing more, nothing less."

His voice has now taken on that slightly sarcastic, mocking quality I've heard before in the duck blind. But never on Saturday, always Sunday morning. And I know now that I will not sway him, yet I do not stop. We will continue like this, and those shared grins of yesterday are now gone. Gone at least until we finally quit talking and pull the decoys or leave the woods. Gone until after a hot shower and a hearty breakfast, we will meet somewhere close to the middle with a smile or a handshake and all will be well again.

"Nothing about suicide? What the hell do you think his promises are? To get back home? What's he going to do, just sit in that woods for a few hours while he gets covered with snow and freezes to death because he likes it? His promises are to his wife and family, and he's not talking about an hour's delay from them. He's thinking of making those woods a permanent resting place. That's what 'the miles to go' before he sleeps is about. Death. Sleep. It's all the same. How can you not see that?" My voice is still a whisper, but it's becoming a hoarse one.

"You're full of it. That proves nothing. Nothing. You can't get suicide out of that poem. I'm so sick of deep, dark literary types overanalyzing everything. You ruin everything," he whispers.

"Look, it's not just me. Clover's prof said—"

"Clover? What the hell kind of name is that?" Bret retorts.

And finally that's enough, and I can take no more. My childlike instincts take over, and I spin around and hit him on the shoulder as hard as I can.

"Doh!"

We freeze in silence as his shout echoes through the cedar swamp, and then we know that it is over. We will see no deer this morning. He smiles, and I laugh, and suddenly it's all over and the cedar swamp is no longer such a dark place.

"C'mon, let's go home," Bret says. "I'm tired."

He extends a hand and helps me get up on cramped legs. I shoulder my rifle and follow his long stride out of my swamp.

—*Greg Frey*

I Am a Fisherman

Standing waist-deep in a lazy current, the water's icy grip claws for access to my skin. It's in luck, as the ankle rip in my "new" waders serves as an open door. Liquid knives embrace my socks in one big hug, and, with nowhere to go, spiral up my calves like serpents, searching for more dry clothing to drench. Each arctic breath I suck in brings me one step closer toward inevitable cardiac arrest.

But I stay in shape for a reason, and it'll take more than a little cold water to send me searching for Davy Jones' locker. Besides, that battle with waders was lost eons ago, so I do what I always do — rationalize the discomfort. The mid-20s air temperature on this fine February morning feels far colder than what's gurgling around my pants. Other than a little squishy sound, and more water weight to lug up and down the stream, it's actually quite pleasant.

In the morning light, frozen fingers locate a fly box. Amazing how cute a stubborn vest zipper can be when interrupted by the slightest material. Even more adorable is the utter loss of fine motor skills when weather and leaky waders cause blood to retreat to the heart in a fruitless quest to keep the brain alive.

With fingers as useful as elbows, I somehow manage to extract said box and celebrate more than I probably should. Holding it like Indiana Jones held the golden idol in the first movie, I pause, exhale, and — in the fit of a massive shiver — proceed to pop the lid off with the subtlety of a hand grenade. The contents — years of begging, bartering, and buying — burst upward and hover, for one brief moment, like Ralphie's infamous lug nut, "*Fuuddge...*" scene in *A Christmas Story*, and scatter to the current. Some flies are still visible as they momentarily swirl around me, but then they quickly vanish despite a myriad of watery scoops that could only resemble someone trying to extinguish a house fire with their bare hands.

Speechless, distraught — and wetter — I spy the box floating in the eddy created by my legs and snatch it before it drifts away. A small yet significant victory for in the corner of one tiny compartment clings

a single fly, my favorite old war horse, the Drunken Doctor, a purple-and-gray streamer with most of the hackle worn off, given to me on a river one cold day ten years earlier. Before vanishing in the mist, the ancient fisherman of few words only told me the fly's name, and that if I took care of it, it'd do its job. And it has, having hooked more steelhead over the years than my skills should render.

With a renewed sense of purpose, and an inner quest to make something out of this morning, I take ten minutes to tie on the Doctor amid bouts of even more intense shivering. At last, I haul several handfuls of line and release them with each false cast until sending ol' Double D — along with a life's worth of memories — to the depths of the far bank. With the morning's petty inconveniences surely in my rearview mirror, I feel a tap and set the hook. *Yes!* Now that's poetic justice for you. Piscatorial perseverance, grit, and determination! I wonder how big he is. He must be huge because he's barely moving.

Actually, he's not moving. At all. Because he's a log.

Losing the Doctor would be a tough pill to swallow, I reason, even if he does go down in the line of duty. But the immediate situation is more pressing given he's my *only* fly. It's deep over there, but I owe him my best rescue attempt, and since I'm already wet up to my knees and my arms are soaked, a teensy bit of water over the tops of my waders will be more than worth it. So, on tip toes, I take one careful step forward.

And fall in.

Headfirst.

Normally in such circumstances, especially in the grasp of life-threatening temperatures, one would leap straight up, almost levitating from the water, and dash back to the truck before hypothermia — or worse — claimed yet another victim.

Not me. I just lay there, bobbing, face down, arms outstretched, wreathed in an amalgamation of candy wrappers, cigar butts, a Ziplock filled with a promising lunch, and a half-sinking roll of toilet paper.

With clarity of thinking that only cold water provides, I ponder while floating that if I let the river sweep me away, I might meet up with some of my lost flies in the first log jam down river. Wouldn't that be a story — nearly drowning as a means of recovering precious angling equipment.

Strangely, the water isn't even cold anymore. It is... refreshing. In an underwater, blurry haze, I search for steelhead speeding by, or just some bait fish. Maybe even a mermaid. Managing to stick a numb finger in the tear in my waders, I realize it's not as big as I thought. Should be an easy patch job when I get home. I clutch instinctively at my prized fly rod, made by an old friend, and laugh bravely — funny how a laugh sounds muffled under water — for a fisherman who still has his fly rod is always in the fight.

Curious the things that funnel through one's head in such cases, when oxygen deprivation and freezing to death should be of highest priority. I wonder what my wife would make for dinner, and wouldn't she be so glad if I returned with just one seven-pounder for the family. I feel the urge to pee, and then laugh — again, so funny underwater — when I decide to just... pee. I mean, I'm already wet, right? I worry about the Doctor, hooked and alone on a deep log in the dark pool across from me. Hopefully I can extract him before I surface. Maybe I'll just swim over there and try. I'll get wet, but again....

Finally, as red stars form on my periphery and childhood vacations begin flashing in slide-show fashion across my vision, I stand up, icy water cascading off my defeated body. Sucking in a large winter's blast of refreshing oxygen, coughing fits ensue for the next five minutes. Stumbling to shore, I trip again, and face plant in a pile of sandy — but thankfully warm — deer dung.

I roll over and wonder if there's enough time to dry my waders, head to town for more flies, and return. Maybe. But tomorrow for sure. Definitely tomorrow.

I can't wait to go again.

I am an optimist.

I am a fisherman.

—*Chris Smith*

The Sentinel

I spent yesterday morning with another dead man. He was hanging from a steel cable, his body backlit by dim light filtering in through a smudged window. Pickling himself in vodka and stepping off a chair was his solution to despair. Hardly human, his face looked like a waxy, discolored mask. Suicides, murders, car wrecks... after decades on the street, this was hardly my first corpse, and unfortunately, far from the last. "Part of the job," we love to say in police work. "You can quit whenever you want."

True, at least in part. With mortgages to pay and mouths to feed, someone's got to earn a living, too. We train. And train. And train. But none of this prepares you for the ghosts that linger behind. Bawdy jokes become coping mechanisms — no disrespect, just gallows humor in the most literal sense. Laughter preserves sanity, or so it seems, proving no one's affected — except we're all perjurers in a courthouse of lies. Psychologists speak of PTSD, acute stress, anxiety, whatever... medical jargon aside, the human psyche only bears so much. In each case, trauma is the perpetrator, and ignorance, a capital crime.

Thank God for dogs. They are what we aren't; they see what we can't; and they listen when no one else will. If they aren't proof of Divine Intervention, what is?

Winston was a field-trial washout, an English setter that never held his tail just right, which is how he came to live with us. Our lumbering Labrador had recently passed on to happier hunting grounds, which left our family searching for a smaller setter. With Winston barely tipping the scales at forty pounds, he fit the bill perfectly — never mind the fact that cops usually prefer protective breeds like shepherds, pits, or rotties. Winston's soft soul makes him a great pal, but a mighty poor guard dog.

But this tri-colored powder keg's got it where it counts. He's driven and debonair, a real demon in the field. His blistering pace burns up the aspens with all the fire and slash of his breed. Making game, his tail transforms into a whirling dervish. Locked on, he stops, rigid and poised, a motionless monument to the wonders of wingshooting. *Right there,* his brown eyes insist, rolling backward. In these moments, the woods sizzle like a high-tension wire, and the blood roars in my ears.

A career surrounded by death and suffering prompts some deep soul-searching. *Why do bad things happen to good people? What about my people? Are they safe? How can I keep from letting this eat me alive?* Unfortunately, answers prove elusive, and questions beget endless others.

A blood-sport like hunting seems like it would further confuse the issue, but the opposite's actually true. Maybe it's because killing plays such a minor role in hunting, or as Spanish philosopher Jose Ortega y

The Sentinel

Gasset noted: "One does not hunt in order to kill; on the contrary, one kills in order to have hunted."

And so we venture out, Winston and I, roaming endlessly among aspens and alders. Leaving the pavement and pain in the city, I trade a fully automatic Colt carbine in favor of a light, 16-gauge double. Its case colors have softened to gray and the walnut stock bears scars from decades afield, but nothing is better suited for birds that fly hard and fall easy.

October brings woodcock by the score, offering a sure limit during the flights. Most days we're content to point and flush, but occasionally we bag a brace for the table. Few meals honor autumn like rare, roast woodcock and an earthy red wine. Later in the season, the brushy margins harbor grouse. Cagier than their long-billed comrades, ruffs prefer flushing wild to sitting tight. Approached with caution, they'll freeze, trusting cryptic coloration to keep them hidden. Misses are common, but occasionally we score, and later, dine like kings.

Watching Winston run, I'm reminded of words written by Guy de la Valdene: "I have a desire to own an all-age, field-trial dog, a crackerjack flamenco dancer with quick feet, a flaring nose, and a whale-bone rib cage; a dog that owns the ground it runs on and the wind on which birds fly. I want a dog whose casts give reason to the landscape, a dog that shakes at the delirium of discovery, and imposes on birds the fortitude of its resolve."

Field-trial failure or not, Winston embodies all that and more, but back home, he passes idle hours beside the wood stove. Any human who slept half as much could conquer the world.

"Haven't you done anything all day?" chides my wife, shaking her head and smiling. At first glance, it appears he hasn't, but Winston's poker face is strong. In truth, he's a shadow, padding quietly about the house, ensuring nothing's out of place and no one's out of sorts. His keen ears are tuned to abnormal sounds: the crinkle of plastic from a chip bag, the whisper of running shoes being laced-up, the crunch of strange footsteps coming up the sidewalk.

Sometimes in the silence, my mind wanders back to the bizarre chaos of police work. Anxiety creeps in like a masked intruder, an enemy immune to punches, taser-probes, and hollow-point bullets. That's when Winston springs into action as the protector, snarling and baring his fangs, more wolf than domestic dog, a savage beast no delinquent would ever dare tangle with. A formidable foe that few irrational anxieties can compete with.

But that's only how *I* see him. In truth, my mild-mannered setter hasn't done anything more than lay a soft head on my knee. Either way, the intruder is vanquished, and order is restored. From that lens, Winston's a far better guard dog than anyone gives him credit for.

—Jon Osborn

Peace to All Who Enter

Mosquitoes are the worst part of early goose season. I can deal with the heat while hunting, provided it's not dangerous for the dog; in fact, it's quite satisfying to gulp down ice water on the tailgate after working up a sweat in the woods. There's a simple solution to the swarms looking for a late-summer snack, but I just can't bring myself to lather up the bug spray on a hunting trip. Fishing, sure — my vest and ballcap carry their own aura of Deet, and I only ruined one fly box before learning the lesson that plastic and bug dope don't play nicely.

But it's been nine months of waiting for September 1st and the commencement of another hunting season. The swatting and slapping and welts are worth it, a princely sum eagerly paid in order to again carry a gun and a flicker of hope through the forest.

And most especially back into The Bottoms.

Chris strode ahead of me, finding his way through the woods as if in a trance, following some unseen compass taking us directly to the blind on Goose Island at one end of the marsh. We'd hunted The Bottoms for three years and, having sole permission to hunt the private slough, felt like we owned it. We'd get up and move with the birds; take long walks to find where the ducks and geese fed or loafed; make smoky, birch-bark fires on the hillsides to warm up; and snooze under a dazzling umbrella of aspen and maple leaves. The Bottoms was our own slice of tax-free, waterfowling heaven.

I wish we would've known that stuffy September morning was to be our last hunt there.

We whispered while we walked, listening for ducks but, more importantly, tuning our ears to the faraway honks out in the marsh. The Bottoms split into two main portions: a primary flooding with scattered islands on one end, and the timber and shrub-cluttered marsh on the other. The woods cleared onto a hillside bordering the flooded timber, and we stopped talking. Black Labrador Maggie frolicked and bounced in circles down the hill and leaped into the narrow channel we needed to wade across to reach Goose Island, but Chris paused and gazed skyward. Orion fought overhead. Always a good sign to set the decoys out underneath Orion the Hunter, provided he disappears under a blanket of clouds come shooting time.

Maggie waked the water like a black muskrat paddling across the channel, climbing onto dry land, shaking, and checking over her shoulder to see what took us so long. She bounded toward the "blind" — nothing more than bracken ferns on an open hillside — while Chris and I navigated deadfalls and blowdowns in the darkness. Upon first discovery, we called it Deadfall Island because of the littering of dead oaks and maples. But the previous season, I dropped a passing goose while Chris was on a stroll, and the bird smacked dead on the island. He hollered from the other end of the marsh and held up a wood duck that fell to a shot I'd heard from him. I reached down and grabbed the goose. He told me later he didn't know which was bigger, the goose or my grin. The name Goose Island stuck.

Dawn's rainbow greeted us — a wash of yellow, orange, blue, and purple supporting a crescent moon. A few minutes after shooting time, the ducks began to move, and Chris and I trembled, picturing the duck season a month away. Mallards banked and cupped and tore away again, teal crisscrossed like a swarm of songbirds, and the whistling of wood duck wings drowned out the mosquitoes for a few glorious moments. Easily the most ducks we'd seen in a single, ferocious morning flight, and then they were gone, and all fell silent, and we wondered if The Bottoms itself had breathed life into the shadows and bewitched us.

The geese slept in. We're not obsessive goose hunters. Sure, we like seeing the big birds set their wings and coast in on autopilot, and we cherish their honking while they pass overhead and herald a new spring. But geese are bonus birds for us, taken as a sidelight to ducks. The early season finds us chasing them more for the fact that we can be out there again — the stunning early mornings, a truck full of decoys, spastic Labs eager for the promise of a retrieve, the anticipation of shouldering a gun to feel the sharp pang of recoil. It wouldn't matter what bird season opened on September 1st — we'd be there.

In the calm morning, my brother and I lounged on the hillside sipping coffee much too hot for the day, but that's where coffee is supposed to be sipped.

"Remember our first opening day here?" Chris asked.

"How could I forget?" I said. "Started out at the Island off Old Mission, and you got a gadwall and me a big greenhead. Then we come here, and Dad gets a wood duck and two mallards, and you get your first drake wood duck." My mind camera-flashed to the pictures stuffed in my journal. I snapped one of Chris when he received his wood duck from Mags, and the awe on his face at the bird's beauty is frozen on that piece of paper forever.

"And you made a fifty-yard shot on that black duck," he said.

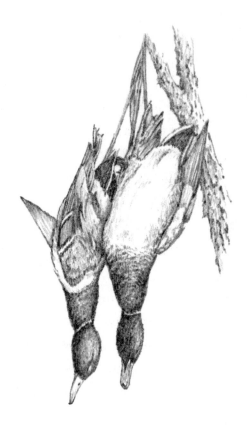

Far-off honks made us hush, but they subsided in the main flooding a couple hundred hidden yards away. Mags sat up, but she relaxed again when the simple noises of the marsh returned.

"That first year, I skipped every Wednesday from college and came out here to shoot two drake mallards. Then I'd sit and wait for a black duck and take pictures. Two drakes, every Wednesday." Chris grinned. "I never would get that black."

We both viewed our education as important but sometimes a deterrent in appropriately appreciating a duck marsh or alder cut or salmon run. Dirtying your hands expands your knowledge better than books at times. Most times. Surely our teachers would want us to become more well-rounded individuals, but we were never brave enough to remind them of that. Rather, we made sure to have a sickly face, a note from Dad — never Mom — and a walk suggesting we might bolt for the bathroom at any instant.

"I'm taking a walk," Chris mumbled. With Mags leaping ahead, he ambled off for the mainland. I leaned back, tipped my tan Filson hat over my eyes, and drifted into memories of past hunts at The Bottoms.

The first duck I ever called in — a beautiful mallard that responded to my one, lone quack. He'd been circling, me too nervous to call. Chris is the calling expert, but he'd taken a stroll to sneak on some birds funneling in to the leatherleaf and cattails a few hundred yards and two hills away. I stayed silent, too afraid of squeaking on the call, but as the mallard turned to leave, I didn't see the harm in trying. The one quack convinced him, and he hit a wall, back-pedaled, and dropped without hesitation. His orange feet swinging to the side for leverage, he slide-slipped almost completely out of the pattern on the first shot; the Model-12 pumped smoothly, and the second shot connected. He seemed to fall forever, tumbling end over end and landing in a geyser. Chris returned and gave Mags a line, and I took the bird from her. Serious tutoring in the art of duck calling started after that. No one rode in the car with me for months.

Memories melted away, shifted form, and took another shape. Fog. Heavy. Another early goose season, only Mags and me. Without much hope, I set out six decoys, trying to compete with the two hundred or so not more than a lazy flyball to left field away, but in the pea soup, anything in the air is fair game — just need to *sound* like a whole bunch of geese. Six emerged from the fog, locked, feet out. I still don't know where those two shots went as the birds departed unscathed.

For all the shots a hunter will miss over the course of his lifetime, there's a pinnacle of accumulated misses that eventually leave him with no expectation of bagging a bird. Oddly enough, it actually makes the trips more enjoyable: If you don't assume you're going to hit every bird you shoot at, you won't be disappointed missing, and the hits will be wildly memorable. I reached this summit ridiculously early in my hunting career. But lying on my back on Goose Island, thinking about those foggy Canadas, those two misses still stung. It would've been my first goose.

Dad and Chris, however, rarely miss. Instances at The Bottoms danced before me, and I again watched them stand, side by side, and tumble matching wood ducks. Or when two shots rang out through the marsh and two geese in a large flock fell… minutes after they told me to go sit under the flight lane the birds took the morning before.

As a family, we take turns shooting while duck hunting when the opportunity arises. Who will stand and shoot is decided upon before birds even show up, all things being equal and safety considerations, well, considered. It is a final measure of respect for the bird and the hunt — *not* to send a wall of steel into the sky and hope for a collision. More importantly, it's our way of squeezing every drop out of an individual experience, and to know, for certain, that a falling bird is "ours," as if we can ever fully possess a thing so wild. One person rising to shoot is a personal experience — death being perhaps *the* most personal experience — and if a miss is made, so be it, and let it be a clean miss. A raw October morning the year before, rising behind the green chicken-wire fenced blind, I still heard Dad whispering in my ear to pick out the drake mallard in the group of four passing overhead. The greenhead that fell next to the blind was the only one in the bunch while we tracked the birds and said, "Hen, hen, hen."

Another time alone made me smile. Expanded my knowledge from the books again one weekday after my senior retreat in high school. The three-day experience had left me spiritually moved, and it only felt proper that I completed it in the heart of God's country. A large greenhead provided the instruction I needed while reflections of the retreat and uncertain college plans kept me company. The soul-stirring shot still echoes through the memory.

I opened my eyes and gazed off the end of Goose Island, cursing silently under my breath when I remembered my swim one cold October day. Good friend Greg Frey and I sat at the main flooding one evening, and I crippled a mallard out of a large flock. He coasted back into the flooded timber, and I tore off after him. Mags and I searched but came up empty.

Coming back through the murky, waist-deep water, I put all of my weight on a submerged stick pretending to be bottom — imagine my surprise when it broke to reveal a rather deep hole. Holding my gun up with one hand and paddling with the other, I struggled to find solid footing, the frigid water beginning to fill my waders and drag me down. Greg's chuckles and snickers as he watched me walk back, drenched to my neck, prompted a flurry of expletives. I made a fire to dry off and warm up and took some solace in the fact that Greg missed both barrels at the flock, and that earlier, I took my first ringneck on a fast, decoying shot.

Honks woke me from my remembrances of birds and hunts at The

Bottoms. I watched through squinted eyes as Chris held still at the peak of a hill overlooking the main flooding, a lone sentry goose approaching, a flock of about a hundred birds close behind. Chris honked frantically, and the bird locked and lowered. I heard the crack from his side-by-side after the big goose began to fall, and the rest of the flock flared back to the flooding. A black blur raced toward the fallen bird.

It was the last bird he ever shot at The Bottoms.

When hunting private land, it's always nice to stay on good terms with the landowners. So, arriving home, Chris phoned them and offered the goose. I'll never forget the look on his face after he hung up. The Bottoms had been sold. To some duck hunters. And they weren't going to allow us access. Hunting at The Bottoms was finished.

Chris left that evening to pick up the duck decoys we left stashed along the trail year-round but more to say goodbye. I declined. He'd discovered The Bottoms by himself, and I thought he should leave it the same way.

On our first trip out there to set up a blind for our maiden hunt, we sat at one section of a trail that spilt the marsh and watched hundreds of wood ducks cross in gun range overhead, filtering into a small roosting pond, flitting like bats feasting in a thick summer evening. And I remember, when we reached the car, turning back to the forest. About fifty yards of plowed field spread before the trail, and the only way to find the entrance into the forest was by using the two large maples standing guard on either side as landmarks. Their branches hung low, framing the entrance to The Bottoms and the darkness beyond in a wide arch, like the entrance to a cathedral. It bid peace, peace to all who should enter to enjoy the sanctuary within. A cathedral is a good description of The Bottoms. Sacred.

The fall prior to losing The Bottoms, Dad and I took the final trip of the duck season there. Chris was off at college, a rare time just Dad and I hunted ducks together. In the heavy fog, all remained still. Hardly anything moved, except for the four suzies I called in, which we let go. But the beauty of The Bottoms, even in the mask of fog… intoxicating. And as we packed up the decoys and made our way to the trail to leave, Dad turned to the flooded timber and said, "I think I will miss this place." He raised his nose to the sky, closed his eyes, and took in a long breath one last time, locking away the scents and sounds and sights of the woods and the marsh and the birds and the memories to keep him warm on the blustery days ahead. He exhaled slowly and opened his eyes. "Yes. Very much so."

Lying in bed, sick from losing the opportunity ever to set foot among The Bottoms' forest and hills and marsh again, those words came back to me. Yes… I will miss that place. Very much so.

At The Bottoms, I grew to appreciate and cherish the world of duck and goose hunting and the birds taken — and more importantly, the ones that remain. The mallards and blacks jabbering their quacks and highballs and chuckles; the wood ducks and their banshee squeals; the air shredding through the primaries of divebombing ringnecks and streaking teal; the hundreds of geese, like guardians of the marsh, honking on their journey, telling the old story of Autumn. Yet it was more than all these. Birch-bark, pine-twig fires that blackened the face. Sunrises and sunsets. The trees set ablaze in October. Walking out under Orion. The hospitable ruffed grouse flushing on the trail in the same spot year after year.

And no matter where I may hunt, whenever I hear or see the birds or lower my face into a delicate fire for warmth, I will go back to The

Bottoms. And I'll sit once more on the wood stumps in our blind or lounge on the hillsides, waiting for — and not waiting for — something to fly by.

In my mind, I will go back.

—Jake Smith

Help Wanted

From behind the Orvis shop counter, my heart skipped a beat, or maybe doubled its pace. It's hard to tell the difference when you are in love. It was there I met Sarah. She had an English setter, a windsurfer, and a really cool dad. She also liked to write books and watch Lake Michigan sunsets. Sarah was the girl I had been waiting for the entire 19 years of my existence.

Quite frankly, it had been a long, painful wait.

It was the summer of 1989, and the world was spinning. The Exxon Valdez had just dumped 240,000 barrels of oil in Prince William Sound. George H.W. Bush held up a bag of cocaine purchased across the street from the White House and promised to spend $7.9 billion on the war on drugs. The first of twenty-four Global Positioning Satellites reached orbit, and the unemployment rate had just dropped to five percent, the lowest since 1973. But I still didn't have a job. Or a girlfriend.

The world had big problems, but I was more concerned with my own. My freshman year at college had brought all things into question.

Were there really such things as answers, or was life just full of questions, one leading to the next? Computer identity theft wasn't even on the radar. How could someone steal my identity when I was still trying to figure out who I was?

The one thing I did know was loneliness. Honorable loneliness, which is different than outcast loneliness, but the result is pretty much the same. Trustworthy, compassionate, sensitive, loyal. Don't let anyone tell you those qualities are blessings. Not when you're 19. Student council president, most likely to succeed, I was the guy girls would call when they had problems. Usually ones with the abusive morons they found so appealing. My father, a high school guidance counselor who rarely drank and never swore, asked me about it one day while driving home from school together.

"So, how's it going? You seem a little down."

I shifted in my seat. Looked out the window.

"Okay, I guess."

"What about girls. Do you like anyone?"

"Kind of. I've got lots of girl friends, just no girlfriend. They like me. They tell me lots of stuff. They say I'm like a brother to them…"

"But you'd really like to just get in their pants."

Holy cow! A psychic! How did he know? Are you supposed to admit that to your dad?

"Uh… yeah, pretty much."

Luckily, life had given me male friends and good counsel. The first came in the form of my high school buddy, Mike, who moved into the family cottage as we searched for summer jobs in Traverse City. We had been inseparable since we met in junior high, which was a puzzle to everyone who knew us. I lived in the woods, hunting and fishing. Mike lived in the basement, watching movies and listening to records.

How hard could it be to separate an outdoorsman from a technophile?

The black flies kept us inside as the mid-May leaves unfurled outside. Hours were spent listening to cassette tapes and searching the classifieds for a summer job. The idleness was bad, but the black flies were worse, so finally I brought our aluminum rowboat into the living room so I could caulk the leaky seams. That may have been a terrible idea because it got in the way of Mike's TVs, and caulk is really hard to get out of carpet. The carp and smallmouth bass would be cruising the flats of Grand Traverse Bay soon. The boat had to be ready. But before that could happen, a call came from The Rainbow, a restaurant just down the road, offering a classic bait and switch. The bait was waitering, with big tips, but bussing tables and washing dishes was the switch. After a long night up to my elbows in greasy water and floating pizza crusts, another call came in.

"This is Jim Colombo from Streamside Orvis. You applied for a job. I wondered if you'd like to come in and talk about it?"

I paused. Was this some sort of cruel joke? A test of my integrity?

"Jim, thank you. I'd really like to, but I've already taken another job. I wish I had only known."

"I understand, but if you change your mind, let me know."

I hung up the phone. Mike looked up from the sofa where he was eating another bowl of Ben and Jerry's and watching MTV on the three TVs he had stacked atop one another.

"What was that all about?"

I told him.

"So why don't you take the other job? It's your dream job for crying out loud. You'll actually get paid to work at a fly shop."

"But I gave The Rainbow my word. I made a commitment."

"You worked one night. Frey, you're an idiot."

The next day I collected the $32 The Rainbow owed me, absorbed their disgust with the help that's available these days, and called Jim back at Streamside Orvis. Thank goodness he had the same problem as The Rainbow, but his was about to get worse because he hired me.

Jim Colombo had helped run the Triangle X in Wyoming for 16 years. He'd packed horses, tied flies, rowed rafts down the Snake, and been the head chef at elk camp. He'd guided heads of state and hard-working guys who saved all year for the trip. At Streamside, Jim taught me how to cast well. More accurately, he taught me how to teach others to cast well. (There was only so much that could be done with a reject dishwasher.) He taught me that big trout can often be found in small water, and that it's okay to put movement on a dry fly. When guiding, do most of the meal prep in private, but leave just enough for the guests to appreciate your hard work. Most importantly, he taught me how to speak your mind, albeit tactfully.

We were guiding a corporate trip of about twelve anglers from a big gas company. He had just thrown the steaks on the grill when one of the clients walked up, beer in hand, many multiples of that in the belly. He raised an eyebrow and peered down at Jim.

"Your fire's a bit hot, isn't it?"

I heard a short intake of breath. Jim squinted up from the portable grill. He smiled and began a joke, but there was a slight edge to his voice.

"You know, when I go hunting, I don't take a compass. I just take a portable grill."

"Oh yeah? Why's that?"

"Because if I get lost, all I have to do is fire up the grill and somebody steps out of the woods to tell me how to use it."

The client melted back into the crowd like fog on an August morning. I nearly peed my pants.

But Streamside was only half the equation. J Michaels Fine Men's Apparel was the other half. Two completely contrasting stores shared a single check-out counter that met in the walkway between them. They were owned by a man from Steamboat Springs who pretty much let us do whatever we wanted. Technically, Jim ran both stores, but everyone knew that Rich was the master of J Michaels. Tall, gray, thin, elegant smoker. Rich would stroll the halls of the resort, lips pursed, head swiveling, cigarette in one hand and the other bent at a right angle to his hips.

While Jim taught me how to find my way out of the woods, Rich taught me that cotton shrinks seven times over its lifetime, only an amateur folds a sweater with the arms crisscrossed, and always close the zippers on your khakis when washing or they'll abrade the rest of the load. Rich put little masking tape flags on his pens so they didn't roll off the counter. He lived alone with his dog, Lally. Three years later, when Rich died, Jim called me at school, and we cried on the phone together.

To balance Rich's elegance and refinement, Jim hired Larry. He may have overcompensated. At first it was just Larry. Ex-military (Air Force, I think), a clean tiger stripe fatigue jacket was high fashion. If you asked Larry what he did in the military, he wouldn't outright lie, but depending on his answer on any given day, you'd leave with the feeling he was somewhere between secret agent and head of European Central Command. I'm pretty sure he fixed airplanes. A renaissance outdoorsman, Larry had an opinion on everything, and he wasn't afraid to share it.

After twenty minutes extolling the virtues of Orvis's $400 multiplier reel, my customer would head to the counter to pull the trigger.

That's when Larry would intercept him.

"I dunno, guy." Larry'd suck in his breath, simultaneously shaking his head and making a disapproving clicking sound with his tongue. "Those things are heavy. Had one once."

"Oh, really?"

"Yeah, now for the money…" And the next thing you'd know, Larry would downsell a millionaire a $39 die-cast piece of crap because after all, "Until you get into the big fish, a reel's really just line storage."

But it got better. He'd caught walleyes on a fly rod. On the surface. He'd been pinned down behind his squad car as bullets popped the tires. During the early goose season (I think Labor Day), he crawled over a dune in his ghillie suit and surprised a couple on the beach near Glen Arbor. We all got pretty sick of it, but Larry was so darn convincing, you never *really* knew for sure.

One day Jim ran into the break room where I was eating a peanut butter and jelly sandwich. He was breathless.

"You've got to see this!"

"What?"

"Larry's talkin' German to these people!"

"No way…"

And he was. There in his debonair tiger stripes, Larry leaned against the fly bins and conversed freely with a distinguished European couple.

"Wo bist du zum Essen rausgekommen?"

"Der Biergarten."

"Aber darf ich etwas besseres empfehlen?"

But *of course* he had dined at The Beer Garden. And obviously he had a finer recommendation. Larry made James Bond look like a cur.

After that it was Amazing Larry, and we believed him. Every single word.

Somewhere in the midst of all this, I confided my troubles to my older friends at the Orvis shop. Surely, they would know what to do. They didn't. Instead, we started the Orvis Poet's Society to document life's tragedies. Little torn scraps of Streamside letterhead began to appear on the storage room wall like mold on the grout of a dirty shower. The writing was kind of gross, too.

Sanctuary (Me)
Away from this ache,
I can't avoid.
Leaving it behind
The powerful outboard thrusts me out to sea
Where among surging swells
And battling kings
You are lost.

Ode to a Bruise (Rich – on a herpes virus outbreak on my nose after getting a sunburn)
Greg Frey – say goodbye
He's leaving with a teary eye.
He'll return
I suppose.
We're hoping with a better nose!

Treat 'Em Right (Jim)

Summer comes
And quickly goes.
Greg fell in love
And now he knows.
Fishing is more fun.

Amazing Larry didn't write poems. But I'm quite sure he edited and revised most of Hemingway's later work. Clearly, I needed better advice.

Jim finally offered some.

"Quit chasing after all these super athletic models and find a girl who likes the same things as you do. They're out there, you know."

Enter John Oakes, renowned cardiologist and fly fisherman. Weathered, strong, and athletic, John was the consummate bachelor and adventurer. He frequented the shop, telling stories of exotic places and buying pretty much whatever he wanted. Guides and doctors have a symbiotic relationship. They both look to the other for what they want to be, or think they should be. The main difference being that when a doctor's car breaks down, it doesn't start a cascade of events that ends in the loss of his job and bankruptcy. John had hunted with Corey Ford and somehow carried the experience and authority that my fellow poets did not. I liked John, looked up to him in fact. One day John introduced me to his good friend, Porter Williams who, conveniently, was the father of Sarah Williams.

Porter had a cottage on Deepwater Point, just down the road from the shop. Being a weekend warrior from Indiana who only did battle in northern Michigan several times a year, Porter was interested in my salmon fishing knowledge. I was interested in his daughter.

"Truth be told, there's not much to it. If the fish are there and feeding, they'll hit. Your rig matters, but not that much."

"Well, I'd much appreciate it if you'd go fishing with me and show me what you know," Porter said.

"I'd be happy to."

A few days later, I met him at his humble cottage on the bay. Porter smoked a pipe, the sweet smell of tobacco drifting in the air, his deep voice telling stories of bird dogs and double guns like a rustic Santa. His wood-paneled station wagon had oak gun drawers that slid out from under dog crates. He made them himself. The cottage was small, and the Boston Whaler was worn. Porter sold seed to Midwestern farmers. He was a man I could relate to.

We trolled for an hour or so as the sun dropped, orange across the bay. Like my own dad, Porter was a really good guy, and I hadn't even met his daughter. The attraction to him as a father-in-law was an undeniable fringe benefit.

When Sarah and I met, it was easy. We walked about the resort, checking out the casting ponds and admiring the view of the bay from the glass-walled lounge on the seventeenth floor of the tower. Conversation was light and natural.

"Jess ate all the chocolate chip cookies off the counter this morning."

"No worries. My setter Sam did that once. They say chocolate is toxic to dogs, but Sam's living proof that it's not. He also ate my entire birthday cake minutes before the party. Of course, Sam was nearing 75 pounds, and he had a pretty good tolerance built up for people food. I'm sure Jess will be fine."

"We should go out for coffee sometime."

As the summer waned, I found excuses to swing by Deepwater Point on the way home. There would be John messing around on the windsurfer he kept at Porter's house while Sarah threw sticks in the water for her setter. Fall was coming. Sarah would be leaving for Indiana soon.

Yet the words hung up inside me. She didn't know how I felt about her, at least I'd never said it. They say better to try and fail than to not try at all. Not sure about that. Staring at the candy jar and filling your head with happy fantasies is definitely more fun than reaching in and getting your hand slapped. And besides, this was a big endeavor, not the kind of thing you want to screw up. Who would understand? Who would be my life coach?

John Oakes, that's who. Closing in on 50, he had life experience. Why not ask him to go fishing? Spill my guts. Talk it over on the boat. Make a game plan. He knew Porter, he knew Sarah, and he knew the lifestyle. He would know the right words, the right approach. He would *understand*.

Bachelor doctors always have time to go fishing. The morning dawned still and quiet, with a thin fog veiling the water. I lowered the boat from the hoist, turned the key, and the outboard pushed me across Grand Traverse Bay to John's house on Old Mission Peninsula. He met me at the dock and invited me in for a cup of coffee. The house set on a steep hill, and by the time we climbed the stairs to the third floor, we could touch the treetops. We stepped out onto a tiny deck where a chessboard was placed on a table. There he played remotely against some friend in Seattle. The whole place was immaculate, an entire dwelling paying homage to the likes of one person. Wildlife art, books, double guns, fly rods. Each had its place. Two pairs of waders hung in the mudroom. I stood awed by the castle.

In his disarming chuckle, John dismissed it all.

"Nothing more to see here. Let's go fishing!"

The fog was starting to lift, but not a hint of wind stirred the air. Perfect conversation weather. Amid the quiet thrum of the outboard and the occasional whine of the downrigger wires, we trolled north along the bay. John told the story of the photograph in the national fly-fishing magazine — the one of him bungee jumping off some bridge in South America, an Orvis rod tube clutched tightly in his hands.

"I was terrified. Hardly slept a wink the night before."

Then he looked around as if someone might be eavesdropping.

"To be honest, I left the rod back in the room at the lodge. I didn't want to break it if something went wrong."

Quite certain a broken fly rod would be the least of his worries if something went wrong.

We talked careers, universities, books, bird hunting. Everything except Sarah. It had been two hours of trolling without so much as a release from the downriggers. I had to get to the point. The conversation drifted to a small river nearby where we both night-fished for big browns. He had been there, a few nights ago, with Sarah. There was a strip bar just down the road.

He chuckled again, that boyish, innocent chuckle.

"We stopped at the Crossroads on the way home, and they had this hideous honky-tonk music playing. We sat right down in our waders, had a bite to eat, and then began dancing out on the dance floor, waders and all."

I still didn't get it.

"That sounds like fun. So, are you... like, kind of like an uncle figure to Sarah?"

"Oh no. We're sweethearts." Innocent grin.

My mind exploded. My jaw hit the floor. I stood mute, unmoving in stunned disbelief, not quite sure how to recover from this shocking revelation.

That's when it happened. God, in His blessed mercy, delivered a salmon. Over John's shoulder, a downrigger rod sprang to life, pumping wildly.

"Fish!"

Jumping up from my seat, I grabbed the rod, violently wrenched it from the rod holder and set the hook with three strong jerks.

"Here! It's yours! Keep tension on it, but take your time."

I shoved the rod into John's hands and furiously cranked in the other lines. Soon, everything was in the boat, and I could shut down the engine. That's the fun part, going *mano a mano* with a king salmon. Charters never shut down the engine. It increases the chances of losing the fish. But, by golly, if it was a salmon John wanted, it was a salmon he'd get. The hard way.

Twenty minutes later, laughing and groaning, John brought the fish to the net. One swift blow to the head, a shudder, and its suffering was over. Wish I could have said the same. I put the fish on ice and turned to John. Handshake, congratulations, hearty pat on the shoulder. The usual job well-done.

He studied me for a moment, puzzled.

"You know, when I told you about Sarah, I thought you were having a seizure or something. But then I realized it was just the excitement of the hit." The quiet little chuckle again. "You had me worried for a minute."

"Oh yeah, just the fish. What say we get you home and clean this thing? It's been a pretty eventful morning."

Puppy Love (Rich)
It's over, Rover
Play dead —
You dog.

—*Greg Frey*

New Dog, Old Dog

The boat launch was still a half-hour away. Speeding through a drizzly October morning — and fueled with plenty of hot coffee and the fact that I'd beaten the alarm by an hour — I tried to slow down and enjoy the drive. With age comes, hopefully, an awareness to stop, or at least pause momentarily, to smell the roses. Relishing the hunt to come almost replaces the hunt itself. *Almost*. But as the first good north wind of the month leaned hard on the roadside maples, tearing wet leaves from limbs, anticipation trumped patience, and I couldn't help but hurry a little.

The mood in the backseat was echoed from the kennel as Ruby, my nine-month-old yellow Lab, whined softly. Mercifully not one to carry on, she no doubt also felt the excitement as each turn brought us closer to the pond and, Lord willing, a chance to do what her genetics dictated: fetch ducks. The whining was actually a good sign. Duck season was almost half over, and she'd been connecting the dots the way I hope a pup will in her first year — a tremendous start on the North Dakota prairie, followed by a steady diet of experiences on our home waters of northern Michigan, saw to that. For a duck hunter and dog guy, nothing beats watching the canine lightbulb turn on.

Waterfowl hunting in these parts is typically mediocre at best. Just the nature of our habitat. Plenty of water spreads birds, and a lack of food — wild celery, coontail, wild rice, etc. — means we're in "fly-over" country. Waterfowlers around here are successful by knowing their stuff, being proficient with a shotgun, going as often as possible, and, above all, finding satisfaction in *not* shooting limits. Sure, they happen when the planets align, but all things being equal, we achieve success in other ways, such as jaw-dropping backdrops to hunt in and little to no competition most days. Watching the dog make even one retrieve is icing on the cake.

But today, thankfully, was one of "those" days, when the predicted north wind brought with it a blessed reprieve of a season-long stalled migration. Flock after flock dusted across the makeshift point blind. The rare limit of six ducks took longer that it would have had I been blazing away at everything in range, but, picking shots for easy marks and retrieves, I stretched it out as long as possible to continue Ruby's eye-opening, first-season journey. Still, much sooner than I'd hoped, the gun was cased, and a grateful acknowledgement was offered to The Man Upstairs — no doubt a duck hunter himself — for such a fine morning. Approaching the launch, which was nothing more than a drab interruption in an otherwise spectacularly colored shoreline, the sun made a brief appearance, lighting the swamp maples that lined the bay and warming our chilled faces.

Drives home from such hunts make even the most hardened duck hunters contemplative. But I vault right over this thoughtful state and become an emotional basket case, especially when it comes to my dogs

— or kids, family, friends... many things, really. Knowing my ten-year-old Lab waited eagerly at the door weighed heavily as I pulled down the dirt driveway. It'd been like that all season: me taking the pup out right in front of Mabel — who's body had given up what her mind still knew it could do — and then trying to explain upon returning home, head buried apologetically in her thick neck fur, that she was still my best girl.

Never one to hold a grudge, she simply wagged a happy welcome as I paid homage to the old pro. She held one of the ducks for a while as I hugged her, wondering what she must be thinking. I know they're dogs, and the concept of forgiveness eludes them. But somewhere in those soft eyes, I hoped she understood.

Worried about another injury that might take her from us earlier than we hope, I hesitate to risk one last hunt. Maybe somewhere controlled, where a perfect opportunity will let me hoist those old bones once more into the water for a last retrieve. Probably too much to hope for, but I'm a duck hunter, and each morning holds promise, not regret.

Releasing Ruby, my two dogs sniffed a cordial recognition, one youngster bounding excitedly around the older, grayer one, each happy in her own way. And there's me, a middle-aged hunter, trying to find balance between the two extremes of a vibrant pup at the start of her career and an old friend near the end of hers.

—*Chris Smith*

Common Scents

"Patches smells bad," my kids complain.

I disagree. *What do kids know, anyway?* I wonder, feeling more like an opinionated old codger by the moment. *It isn't just clothes and music! This generation can't even appreciate the right aromas!*

Then again, I'm one of those olfactory eclectics who enjoys an indulgent whiff of unleaded gasoline mixed with oil, organic swamp muck, and skunk-at-a-distance. These outdoorsy fragrances smack of experience and adventure — complex, acquired tastes that urban individuals seldom learn to love. Civilized types who prefer body sprays and eucalyptus water-lily air fresheners should search elsewhere.

"Patches," my old buffalo-plaid shirt, has been my favorite since high school, which hadn't seemed all that long ago — until I did the math. Turns out, nearly three decades have passed since senior year. *C'est la vie*, simply more evidence that there's no friend like an old friend — an adage that applies to bird dogs, people, *and* favorite shirts.

The kids are right about one thing, though. Patches is a perfect nickname. Back in 1993, the checkered shirt was the pride of the L.L. Bean catalog, but now it's a sad swatch of amateur repairs. Scraps of waxed cotton cover threadbare elbows, and amateur whipstitches reinforce unraveling seams and dangling buttons. The ragtag needle-and-thread work is obvious and imperfect. Much-loved, some would say, albeit in apologetic, "Bless his li'l heart" tones.

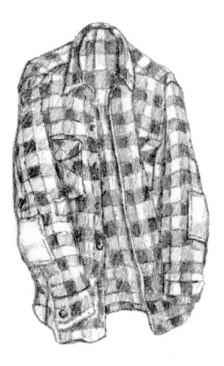

Appearances aside, it's time to clear the air. Patches doesn't smell *bad*. On the contrary, this woolen masterpiece is steeped in history and ripe with experience. And like a cast-iron fry pan or a trusty Weber grill, none of this seasoning was acquired quickly or easily. Decades of time and effort have imparted an aroma that speaks of campfires, chainsaw exhaust, pipe smoke, gun oil, and three generations of wet dogs — in other words, pure bliss. With apologies to Julie Andrews, these are a few of *my* favorite things.

Aromachologists study the influence of odors on human behavior, and they insist our fifth sense — smell — is intricately linked to memory and emotion. While a human's ability to interpret odors isn't nearly as adept as, say, an English setter's, fragrances transport us back in time quicker than any DeLorean ever could, 1.21 gigawatts notwithstanding.

One whiff of old canvas and we're kids again, camped out under the stars in a timeworn Sears and Roebuck pup tent. Or maybe the combined aroma of musty Labrador, marsh grass, and Evinrude exhaust puts us back in the duck boat with Dad. Fresh-cut alfalfa, horse barns, hickory smoke... poignant reminders of places we've been and wish we could return to.

Fragrances aside, Patches is a wonder of modern material. That it remains a viable article of clothing after a third of a century is a testament to the longevity of wool. Come to think of it, good old sheep's fleece has a lot going in its favor. It doesn't pill or fade and retains insulating qualities, even when wet. Its scratchy countenance, however, isn't for the faint of heart. Wool rarely finds favor among weekend wild men and Instagram outdoorsmen obsessed with beard wax, pegged pants, and cozy, synthetic fabrics. But what about those rare, hearty souls who still prefer camping in canvas lean-tos, splitting firewood with double-bitted axes, and paddling cedar-strip canoes? Traditional deer hunters, old-school fly anglers, and classic-minded wingshooters... unite! For us, wool remains the *ultimate* fabric.

When it comes down to it, Patches smells like hunting, which shouldn't come as much surprise. Spend enough time among the alders and briar patches and you wind up a bit tattered, smelling of all the smoky, swampy places you've travelled; all the whiskey you've sipped; all the setters, springers, and Labradors you've passed the golden autumn hours alongside. It's the price — perhaps even the *privilege* — of a sporting life well lived.

Which brings to mind a day last fall. My son Wil and I were heading out to shoot clay pigeons at a local gun club. With the mercury hovering in the high forties, naturally I was wearing Patches. For what it's worth, the kids advertise their unease like a neon sign when I don Patches in public.

"You look like Elmer Fudd, Dad," they insist. Quite frankly, their embarrassment is contagious, making me a bit self-conscious, too. But only for a moment. The feeling passes quickly, replaced by the pride of owning — nay, *wearing* — so storied a relic around town. Snicker all you want, naysayers, I'll be the one standing outside in the chilly mist, comfortable as a canvasback in the sleet.

Later that day, as we were driving past a local greasy spoon, Wil glanced up from his comic book, chuckled, and muttered, "I knew I smelt something." Following his gaze, I noticed a marquee out front that read: FRIDAY NIGHT FISH FRY — ALL-YOU-CAN-EAT SMELT. The kid fancies himself a comedian, but this was, indeed, a witty pun. Besides, in my heart-of-hearts, I felt relieved. For a moment I thought he'd been referring to Patches.

—*Jon Osborn*

A Trifling of Flies

Before a fly rod ever found its way into my hands, I clamped a #12 dry fly hook — a Mustad 94840 — into the jaws of a vise and tied an Adams. Gifted to me a couple of months before moving to trout-infested northwest lower Michigan, the fly-tying kit looked like a hornet's nest of impossible creativity. The photos on the instruction manual's cover might as well have been the sculpted David standing proudly amid a pile of white marble. My first flies were atrocious. But that tiny creation of my own hands, a birth of my imagination into physical form, was enchanting. I pictured my first fat trout hypnotized by it, and daydreamed of a summer on the river with a line dancing around my head and a bent fly rod aching my arm.

I think I lost that Adams to a hungry tag alder on my second cast.

I'd also been promised that fly fishing was an expensive hobby, especially for a beginning caster, so you could save money by tying your own flies. Music to a teenager's ears. I am fairly certain the person who fed me this propaganda was my brother Chris, who is distinguished among his peers as having paid for only seven flies in his entire life and tied seven fewer than that.

Whether because of the addiction to creating or the fervent hope that, thirty-plus years into it, I'll finally realize more bang for my buck, tying flies is simply a part of who I am. While each fly slowly coming together on the vise before me summons a speck of hope that it will never fail, it is more than that. It provides a connection to the river and the fish and all those dazzling trips astream of the past and of those yet to come. I can't help but romanticize the feeling of bringing a trout to hand on a fly that I tied, and looking back at fish caught — both the behemoths and the ankle-biters — I see them more vividly with one of my Royal Soft Hackles or a sleek streamer of my own design in its mouth. A plastic snap box in my fly-tying desk contains a few memorable flies that served their tours of duty in my vest and now rest on their laurels in cozy retirement. I pull them out every so often, see again the day, feel once more the pull on the rod. And if I think carefully, I can remember the feathers and fur and thread spiraling together to create something I didn't know at the time would be luck incarnate.

Finding joy in tying flies isn't limited to those at the end of my line. Giving them as gifts and then, later, finding out that every brown trout in the river turned its nose up at other Hex flies except for my pale-yellow wulff version produces nearly as much gratification as if I hooked the fish myself. It is something Chris often reminds me of while wondering if I have a couple of Royal Coachman Streamers ready for him from his "standing order." I humor him. So does fellow Lost Branch Sportsman's Club member Jon Osborn, who ties a deadly Skunk that bluegill brawl over the instant it hits the surface. Chris likes to think he has Jon and me hoodwinked into giving him free flies with his "starving artist" schtick. I suppose he does. Pity is powerful currency. So is flattery.

I used to sit at my grandfather's old accounting desk and do my homework after walking to their house from school. Back then, the desk was walnut-colored, its circular, antique handles clapping like door knockers when I'd fiddle with them. After Gram passed, my sister Amy stayed with Gramps while completing hospital requirements for her Physician's Assistant degree, and it was Amy who found him unconscious from a stroke that, less than twenty-four hours later, would lead him Home at 82. When she started her family, she took the desk and painted it a couple of different colors — it's black now — but kept those patinaed brass handles. Every time I visited her, I'd twist her arm a little more with a comment about the desk looking out of place in her living room and that she should consider getting rid of it. It only took twenty-five years, but she finally renovated her living room enough that the desk needed a new home. Quite a shock when she opened the back of her SUV one day. She said I finally wore her down.

It is not the most ideal desk for tying flies, but it is for me. The brass handles still clatter when I sift through the drawers. Each clap sends me back to Gram and Gramp's little city house and their den with the shag carpet and my middle school homework, and I smell again the aroma of Gram's black coffee and cheese puffs while she watched her "programs." I think Gramps would be happy it's been a focal point in two living rooms of his grandchildren, and he would've loved to see some of my flies, even though I'm sure he never cast one.

Placing it in our house, I spent a satisfying evening sorting my modest collection of tying materials into the drawers. Flies are made all the more special when created with the feathers and fur of the creatures we pursue, whether through our own harvest or as gifts from friends on the other side of the country. A Hungarian partridge or valley quail feather taken under skies big and wide can be the key ingredient to a pattern. I have enough hair from swatches of special deer for a hundred lifetimes of ugly streamers and hefty bass bugs, but I can't bring myself *not* to save some from my wife's buck or my sons' first does. The wood duck and mallard and hooded merganser flanks from birds retrieved by special dogs; ruffed grouse breast feathers from the last grouse my setter pointed; the iridescent feathers from the neck of a wild turkey I shot with my 16-gauge Fox... each of these a recycling of the natural world that, I'm convinced, infuses the fly with moxie not found in the materials hanging on shop walls and, frankly, just makes me feel better.

At the moment, the clutter on the desk consists of a handful of tying books and magazines. I'm on the hunt for a pair of antique bookends to tidy things up. The old *Index of Orvis Fly Patterns* — a plastic-encased, three-ring binder — started me off on my fly-tying journey. Included in that first kit, the book provided a suitable way of tracking the flies I used most and introduced me to a captivating world of new fish and new rivers by studying the flies. I never knew you could catch a salmon on a dry fly in some parts of the world, or that trout could zero in on something as miniscule as a Trico. The backside of the pages contain my first attempts at documenting inventions that might set my place in fly-fishing legend. Nothing more than scribbles in Sharpie marker. The only one that panned out was a green and gold salmon-style fly that landed Chris a Master Angler class sea-run brook trout in the Kaskattama River flowing into Hudson Bay. I'm sure the fish would've taken a gold earring, so it's not saying much.

Art Flick's 1969 *New Streamside Guide*, gifted to me by a Montana photographer friend, provided some fascinating background on Quill Gordons, Hendricksons, and hatch schedules. Fellow free-fly enabler Jon Osborn secures a slot in my fly-tying library with his *Classic Michigan Flies: 16 Legendary Patterns*, a beautifully illustrated narrative that is more historical than instructional about traditional flies we still tie and fish. And Dick Pobst's handy pocket guide, *Trout Stream Insects*, goes back and forth between the desk and the old wooden Winchester ammunition box in my car that collects all manner of fly-fishing odds and ends during the season. I've consulted it for nearly twenty-five years, and it still coughs up a gem now and then — just last season in the form of *Ephoron leukon*, the white mayfly of late-summer evening hatches.

It is Sylvester Nemes' 1991 book *Soft-Hackled Fly Imitations*, however, that I consider my tying bible. And not so much for its instruction or patterns — for it's almost entirely about Western flies — but rather for its celebration of the *type* of fly: the soft hackle. It was his third book on the topic, and I confess I haven't yet read the first two. But reading his reasoning behind the development of certain soft hackles and the simplicity of the patterns spurred my imagineering of this delicate, practical art form more than any other. Although it's mesmerizing to pore over a kaleidoscope of flies while you sit on the bank, the soft-hackle style — always with a Hungarian partridge or ruffed grouse breast feather — has held sway over our fly boxes. Olive; gray; sulphur; mahogany; the two all-star performers of a gold-ribbed brown and the traditional royal arrangement; an experimental peacock-herled "gnat" version; and, after seeing the *E. leukon* in Pobst's book, an all-white version whose maiden voyage pulled persnickety trout from a rain-splattered river for Jon and Chris when nothing else would. Hex and brown drake imitations will be birthed this winter, though it's been an age since I've spent a night waiting on shark-like browns to emerge from their cutbanks and hunt.

"... *Soft-Hackled Fly Imitations* has finally freed me from the dicta, confines and cultism of dry fly fishing," Mr. Nemes wrote. "Now, I can live and fish without absolutely stiff, spiky, dry fly hackles on my imitations. I no longer have to worry about drag, miscocked wings, flies floating, floatants, size and the ephemeral stages, emerger, dun, or spinner. I can concentrate more on the fun of fly fishing, the end... not the mechanics... not the means...."

After reading Mr. Nemes' description, you're apt to think soft hackles sloppy flies for sloppy fisherman, an insult to the fabled intelligence of discerning trout. But they work. Fish will be finicky with them for color and size and presentation, make no mistake, but I see soft hackles as the offspring of simplicity and magic itself. Simple materials tied sparsely more realistically represent the delicate mayfly we trout fisherman base so much of our angling lives around. They cut through the pomp and circumstance of some of the modern monstrosities being flung across rivers, which no doubt prompt trout to strike out of self-defense. And the allure of a soft hackle lies in its ability to represent nearly all stages of a mayfly's life in a single drift, albeit in reverse — from a dun sitting purposefully on the surface, to an emerger in the film, to a struggling nymph at the end of the drift when drag pulls the fly under. Therein resides the bit of magic every angler desperately searches for.

The old Orvis binder gave way a few years ago to a sketch book where I tried to keep straight my patterns, tying techniques, recipes, and other thoughts. Mercifully, our Labrador Cici — just entering her senior citizen years at the time — saved a future generation from suffering the indignity of looking at my drawings when she casually removed the book from my backpack and shredded it. Journal Number Two now sits out of reach of curious Labradors. I've taken more to documenting and doodling and reflecting about my time on the water and in the daydreams of what another day might hold. Jotting my thoughts and sketches of the flies I never want to forget how to tie is refreshing relaxation, like dunking my ballcap in our hallowed Boardman River and dousing myself on a hot day.

Perhaps the most entertaining part of the books and the histories and the patterns are the names. Not the Black Stonefly or Golden Darter or others that simply restate the name of what it claims to represent, but the intriguing ones that conjure an impression of a backstory that needs to be told. Silver Doctor or Mickey Finn or Crazy Charlie. And I don't know about you, but every time I hear Royal Coachman, I can't help but think of a proper gent driving Cinderella to the ball.

Therefore, when you invent a fly with an eye toward either representing a bug or making something flashy enough to be irresistible, the enjoyment is not only in the concocting but in the naming. Lazily, it could be representative of a color or feather. It shouldn't be something already in use, which is sometimes hard to avoid; as long as it isn't marketed, there shouldn't be any harm in giving it your own twist by adding the name of a favorite dog or a crazy uncle. It shouldn't be something so crude you'd hate to utter it in the presence of gentle strangers. Nothing makes the birds choke on their pleasant chirping more than calling downstream that the fish are taking a fly you've given a name that would make a sailor apologize to his mother. It could be a clever turn of phrase, or a commemoration of an event that transpired when you fished it nameless. In the case of my first invented fly — the

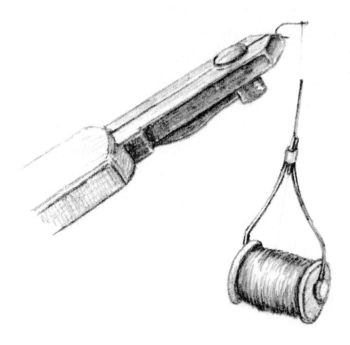

Gypsy Strangler — the name arose from an irreverent short story I wrote as a teenager about a man searching for the mysterious ingredients of a fly needed to catch a mythical trout in order to release a ghost fated to haunt the streambank. I only remember bits and pieces of the story and can't find a copy of it anywhere, but Greg Frey still has the original fly sitting on his nightstand.

 A recent fascination with old-fashioned steelhead flies — whether designed for steelhead specifically or adapted from other wet and salmon flies — drove me to my sketchbook and some dissection of old patterns such as the Skykomish Sunrise and Umpqua Special and Parmachene Belle. No reason I couldn't tweak a little more to design some for our Michigan waters, right? Who cares if I've never caught a steelhead. Bucktail and floss and mylar and hackle and sprigs of duck flank spin around a beautiful spey hook in various color configurations and sit there, waiting for a personality to blossom with the right name. Rocketeer, Kingfisher, Mr. O'Leary, The Plum Lady, Dragon Breath... they all seem pleasing to my eye, if not a steelhead's.

I've given my own twist to other flies, be it a bluegill bug for a hot day on Mom and Dad's lake, or a saltwater shrimp while envisioning a maybe-someday trip to the Bahamas for bonefish. Inspecting a new type of fly — such as one with an articulated joint or trailing a stinger hook — can provide inspiration of variations for our rivers. Other times, catching a cruising fish on a spinning rod with a chunky Rapala will challenge me to replicate the lure with delicate materials to see if the same fish can be fooled on a flimsy three-weight.

Begging forgiveness from Mr. Nemes, I must take exception to the last part of his quote, about the splendor of soft hackles allowing him to "concentrate more on the fun of fly fishing, the end... not the mechanics... not the means...." And I think, if he were to reread it, he might do so himself, too. While his book — and his others before it — most certainly focused on the "means" of fishing, his dedication to the fly, inventing new patterns, testing them on waters across the continent, fiddling with their potions in a pinch-of-this and dash-of-that alchemy, and then writing about it... you can't tell me he didn't find some fun in all that.

In fact, as solitude becomes scarce and fishing apparently something to "win," we *must* discover fun in more places than simply the jaw of a trout if we are to wrest the rejuvenation of our spirit from a world all too intent on crushing it. Tying flies is perhaps the thing I love most about fly fishing. It is not weather-dependent. It doesn't care if someone's in your spot. It matters not if the blue-winged olives or caddis are coming off or if spring rains have swollen the banks. In a hobby where so much is out of our control, tying a fly remains right there in front of you, the hook a blank canvas upon which you are the sole artist. It provides one of the oldest customs of fishing and too-few courtesies seemingly left, that of exchanging a couple of flies with a stranger on the river upon meeting, or when you catch up with a friend after too many years' passing since you last shared a streambank. A hand-tied fly is art and engineering, whimsy and practicality, bits of treasure selfishly guarded one instant and freely shared the next.

For something so small to contain so much — enjoyment, hopes, dreams, imaginations, civility, memory — well, it seems a bit of the Divine leaking into our world. And they might even catch a fish or two.

—Jake Smith

Walk With Me

Some day when you have lots of time to think, such as a hot summer day when your bobber just isn't budging or maybe when you're in a deer blind between the hours of noon and two, ask yourself a question: "If I could do only one outdoor activity, which would bring me the greatest pleasure for the rest of my life?"

Seriously, play the game. God is testing you by taking away, one by one, each of your favorite hobbies, just like he did with Job. Actually, Satan was tormenting Job, but God was letting him do it, so if you ask me, they were in cahoots with one another.

Bluegill fishing over the beds with a fly rod on a warm spring evening?

Gone!

Mallards dropping into the corn stubble as crisp October winds rustle the few remaining leaves?

Gone!

Salmon slamming a glow spoon off the breakwall just as the sunset drops into Lake Michigan?

Gone!

Woodcock rising above the alders as your setter holds tight?

Gone!

But God has mercy, and He stops Satan while you still have one good outdoorsy hobby left. What's it gonna be? What's your one thing that you would hold back? It better be good because it's all you've got until you leave this planet.

Me? I've already thought about it. A lot. It's not even a hard decision because there's nothing running a close second.

I'd keep walking the dogs.

That's right. More than any outdoor pursuit, walking the dogs gets me out into nature two, sometimes three, times a day whereas all of my other outdoor hobbies are seasonal at best and often only a day or two a year at worst. Walking the dogs gets me outdoors in the quiet, still early morning as the day wakes, sometimes at noon when the winds are blowing and I need to clear my head, and again right after dinner when the world is ready to go to bed.

I'm fortunate because we live in a small subdivision surrounded by a couple hundred acres of Walloon Lake Conservancy forest. I've gotten lost, quite literally, exploring the miles of trails winding through old growth beech, hemlock, maple, oak, and once living ash trees. Most of the time the dogs are with me. While my hunting cabin sits two hours away and only gets visited three or four times a year, in my daily walks with the dogs, I visit the cabin often, revisiting old hunts and planning new ones.

While I've owned a pedigreed, field trained English setter who was given to me when I was 17 (the year I learned adults lie) by the president of the Ruffed Grouse Society because Sam was a "slow hunter," and a

German shorthair named Heidi who made the Energizer Bunny look like a sloth, my current compadres do not hunt. At least not game in the traditional sense of the word.

Lily is a small black Scottish terrier (for sure) and a pit bull terrier (we think) mix, and Henry is a white and brown Labradoodle who looks like a springer spaniel that had a bad encounter with an electric fence. Small burs love his soft, fine afro, and they know that he can transport them for miles across the planet. What the burs have not figured out is that they never fall out of his fur. The only way to remove them is to cut them out, where they end up in a softball-sized clump in the garbage can. Henry ends up with a bad-looking haircut.

The two of them remind me of George and Lennie from *Of Mice and Men*. One big, one small. One white, one black. One old and wise, one young and silly. Lily is smart and responsible, her main vice a Napoleon syndrome toward other dogs. Henry is perpetually happy, entertaining himself by attacking the rotary sprinkler and doing cartwheels in the wet grass. He's a lot like Tigger as he bounces and trounces his way through life, which is not a problem if you have a knee at the ready or can spin like a bull fighter. We watch Henry when elderly people are around.

Henry has a dark side though. He chases deer. "Chases" is not actually the correct word. Flushes. Henry flushes deer. You can tell when it's about to happen. He catches a scent, drops his head, and lines out like a rocket; but the pursuit never lasts more than a hundred yards. I can set my watch to him. He'll be back in twenty seconds or less, quite proud of himself. If I catch him thinking about it before his instincts take over, I can call him off. In fact, one time, he and I watched a doe in the neighbor's yard for quite some time. All I had to do was growl, "Henry, don't even think about it." He didn't. So when he flushes one once in a while, I have a hard time seeing the difference between that and a spaniel or Lab putting a bird to flight followed by a short chase.

Not everyone agrees. A bowhunter on the Conservancy trails once warned me about him, saying that he had the right to shoot any dog chasing deer, and that Henry should wear blaze orange. The thought occurred to me that Henry would as likely chase a deer toward a hunter as away from a hunter, but I try not to argue with others when they are armed and I am not. Instead, I bought Henry a blaze orange vest and threatened to kill the man if he ever hurt my dog. I also called a local conservation officer who busted the myth about the shooting of dogs running deer. He assured me that the only person who has a legal right to ever shoot someone else's dog is a law enforcement officer, and even they wouldn't do that because the fallout is just not worth it.

For the last year or so, once Henry turned one, it's been hard to get him out the door for a morning walk anyway. He's not worried about being shot; he's playing tug-of-war with Lily. We stumble downstairs together, both tugging at my hands and at each other, quite literally a tangle of legs and bodies thumping down the stairs. They wait patiently and quietly while I pour a cup of coffee, and when I turn down the hallway toward the front door, the frenzy begins. Lily starts it, grabbing a stuffed animal and thrusting it at Henry. He obnoxiously barks in her face before taking hold of the other end. By this time, I'm waiting at the front door, coffee cup in hand, and the tugging, growling brawl has begun.

"C'mon, time for a walk."

Grrrrr....urrgggh...rrrrrrr!

The growl tug fest grows louder.

I open the door. "You guys coming or not?"

More growls and snarls. This time louder and more determined.

Henry, at least, gives me a glance out of the corner of his eye. Lily is committed to the fight. Henry is twice the size of Lily, but no one is gaining ground. That's one clue this is just theatre and no one really means what they say, kind of like politics these days.

That's when I play my trump card.

"So I'll see you two later. I'm going for a walk." I shut the door, take two steps, and wait three seconds. Then I reopen the door. This strategy always works. Henry finds his Samson-like strength, pulls Lily across the living room carpet, and being the wise one, she lets go before being dragged through the threshold and down three steps. Henry prances victorious across the wet grass or icy snow to the middle of the front yard where he drops the stuffed animal and refuses to pick it up again when we finish our walk.

It's like that every… single… day. The fact that they never tire of this game amuses me, even though it's so darn obnoxious. It puts me in a good mood every morning. We stroll up to the cul-de-sac, Henry ranging through the woods while Lily sticks with me on the edge of the street. We survey the treetops, looking at the light as it hits them, the breeze as it stirs them, the clouds far beyond them, gauging the day's temperament. Then after my coffee cup is drained, my body is loosened up, and the cobwebs are cleared, all I have to say is, "How about some breakfast?" and everyone does an about-face for home.

Night walks are a little more adventurous. Usually we're not alone. About every other year or so, our neighborhood is overrun by thugs who move out from the surrounding forest to claim more turf. They're part of the same gang, one big, unified clan, and they all wear the same color — black, though single members show off their individualism by the amount of white they show in the dark. A lot or a little, it's always a stripe, and they're not after the turf so much as the grubs that live in the turf. That and the incredible, free, fortress-like housing our neighborhood offers by way of twenty-foot-long galvanized driveway culverts. When you step back and think about it, how can you be mad at the skunks? They're doing their best to survive in this world just like we are. Plus, just like grizzly bears and cougars, they make my walks with the dogs a little scary, but in a glad-to-be-alive-skydiving kind of way.

Truth be told, I have a thing for skunks, and next to serpents who really got the shaft no thanks to Adam and Eve, skunks, opossums, porcupines, and coyotes all seem to be on man's naughty list. That strikes me as incredibly unfair. Just because they spray, hiss, have ugly tails, eat trees (so do beavers and a million insects), and eat deer (so do we), these runners-up to the snakes of the world are just doing what

God created them to do in a natural world so much more perfected and in balance than our own human society.

I try to be a patient listener and open-minded to the other half of the population that loves/hates Bush/Obama/Trump/Biden/fill in the leader, but if you tell me you live trap skunks and then throw their blanket covered cage into a barrel of water or a shallow pond, I'm equally liable to throw up, cry, or try to put you in a choke hold. Same with shooting any animal that you don't intend to eat or which is not within seconds of eating your pet, child, or your foot.

So back to skunks and dogs, which are both my friends. You may think I've never been sprayed, and therein lies my smugness. Not true. I lost my most beloved sweatshirt from The Boyne River Brewery to a skunk. (I lost the rest of my clothes, too, but the socks, underwear, and jeans could be easily replaced.) It happened innocently enough. Pulling into the driveway after a late-night October hockey game, I quietly opened the front door so Sammy, our former Labradoodle, could slip out to greet me without waking the rest of the family. Instead of greeting me, he heard the rustle of dry leaves on the edge of the yard and made a beeline for it. I tried to call him back, hoping upon hope that it was just a young deer shuffling through the leaves; but when he returned, clawing at his wet face and bloodshot eyes, I had to face the truth.

My wife came to the door, and just like the scene in *The Rock*, when the rogue soldiers stealing the VX gas drop a container and the leader sadly seals the door on the one man who can't make it out in time, she threw a couple towels out the door, some soap, and a garbage bag for my clothes, then sadly shook her head and turned away. Oh, I've dealt with my share of skunks, and so has Nessa, Tasha, Sam, Heidi, Sammy, and Lily. Henry, as of yet, is unscathed. He's only two. There are three sure things in life: death, taxes, and skunks. It's only a matter of time.

I've put my time in with skunks, and I've grown to appreciate them. I also have learned a thing or two about them. First off, skunks are nice creatures. They don't want to spray you or your dog. And they're pretty good at reading body language and tone of voice/bark of both humans and dogs. If not threatened, they'd just as soon go about their business of living in culverts and digging grubs out of the ground.

Case in point. One night my wife Kristin and I were walking down our wooded neighborhood in early September. Darkness had fallen quickly, so Henry and Lily each wore a glowing LED collar. We were rounding a bend when I realized Lily had disappeared. I looked into the neighbor's yard on the left, and a red light spun rapidly in a four-foot circle. Shining my flashlight toward it, I saw an amused skunk in the middle of the circle, it's tail up as it pivoted on its front legs and kept its rear end aimed at Lily as she ran circles around it. Lily wasn't snarling or barking, and the skunk obviously didn't want to spray or it would have already. Kristin did the logical thing by turning and sprinting up the street with a scared Henry at her heels. Once again, I was left behind the locked door with the VX gas. I called Lily over to me, the skunk lowered its tail and went back to searching for grubs, and we all headed home none the smellier.

Most encounters follow a similar pattern. Spot the skunk before your dogs try to annihilate it; say something friendly and calm like, "How's the grub hunting going?"; keep walking; and all will be well. My walks with the dogs always seem enriched by a friendly encounter with a skunk.

Summer is coming to an end, and school's about to start. My days on the water will come to a screeching halt, and my trips to the hunting camp will be few and far between. But my walks with the dogs will keep me connected to the natural world every day, and that will keep me connected to the games I long to play with rod and gun in hand, even if it's just a half-hour mental escape during the workday. For that, I'm forever grateful.

—Greg Frey

The Trapper's Cabin

He discovered it one day like so many of his precious spots — while lost amid the impenetrable swampland of Michigan's Upper Peninsula.

Cutting class from a local university, he'd driven west two hours to a clearcut he'd bird-hunted the previous fall. Donning hip waders and uncasing the hand-me-down shotgun, he loaded his father's old backpack with as many shells as he felt like carrying, water, survival kit, blanket, and a couple of sandwiches. Over the other shoulder, he slung a mesh bag of six, aqua-keel mallard decoys, knowing he'd regret not having them only slightly more than lugging them along the upcoming journey. Following a twisting logging road where the map suggested a creek would lead to a pond, he was confident of stumbling upon a mallard Valhalla. Well, hopefully a few, anyway. To a college kid living on cafeteria food, a duck dinner qualified as five-star cuisine.

The creek was right where it should be, but after navigating its banks for several hours, no pond was in sight. Then the water started spreading delta-like around an array of islands, and he was lost by late afternoon. Thankfully, Dad's compass had gotten him out of trouble before, so he took a reading and plodded along the branch with the strongest current.

He spent that first night curled up under an old cedar tree, the chilly October wind partially blocked by a gnarly blowdown. A birch-bark and cedar-limb fire offered nominal warmth and kept the critters in his imagination at bay. No one would worry — he often left for long weekends without warning his roomies, and his parents were accustomed to going days without hearing from him. Fiercely independent, he used every bit of the long leash they nervously offered.

Waking up hungry and half-congealed but otherwise no worse for wear, he proceeded north. When the sun was highest, the opening he hoped was a body of water proved to be an old beaver meadow, evidence that a pond or lake had once been there. His wildlife classes reminded him of the successional stages such a place had gone through on its millennia-long journey to becoming a beech-maple climax forest, not to mention that crossing the middle wouldn't be smart — U.P. bogs were the Bermuda Triangle of the North. Skirting the swamp's edges and picking up the creek again in the next clearing, he hit pay dirt — forty acres of open water, with a long point sticking out into the middle.

At first, the site of the old cabin was deflating. Had he come all this way to find someone's property? But upon closer inspection, he found it abandoned — for years, by the looks of it. A broken window, cracked by the sagging frame; an old bee's nest under one eve; bracken ferns growing up through the wooden steps; the top of a nearby white pine that had busted off and caved in a small corner of the roof.

Plenty of black bears roamed those swamps, so he approached the place with enough caution that when a raccoon bolted from the open front door, his yell was stifled by nervous relief. Entering slowly, the ambient air smelled fresh rather than musty, ventilation courtesy of the open door and hole in the roof. In the far corner was an old bunk where a mouse-shredded mattress clung to a few rusty springs; against an adjacent wall lay a '50s-style kitchen that offered a view of the pond; behind him, a pretty solid-looking wood stove. The chimney appeared in decent shape so much that he envisioned a roaring fire to warm his frozen digits.

Several odds and ends adorned an old table: *Fur-Fish-Game* magazines, similar to those he'd seen in his father's collection as a kid, and an old canvasback decoy, the head of which lay on the wood floor. He immediately snatched it up as a collector would a dust-covered Purdy shotgun at a garage sale. Carefully appraising the ancient deke, he noticed a couple of shot holes, sure signs that whoever lived here hunted, probably for food, first; but the way the decoy sat, he imagined the owner must have loved waterfowling as he, too, was learning to love it. Beneath the lead-weighted keel, burned into the cedar block, was one simple word: *Sam*.

In another corner, propped against a worn, hickory-handled ax, rested two traps, the same conibears a professor taught him were perfect for taking beavers. Connecting the dots, he envisioned this gentleman a true sportsman, a trapper and hunter who lived off the land, as so many aspired to do yet rarely achieved. But what had driven him to seek such solitude? Family? Work? Perhaps Sam served in WWII and simply desired to live out his days in peace.

Since his own grandfather was a B-24 waist-gunner who flew missions over Germany, he chose to believe that last option... a war hero who said goodbye to the world to scratch out his remaining years from this beautiful country, on his own terms. Or maybe it was because he could see himself doing the very same thing someday.

He noticed a tweed hat hanging from a nail, with the remnants of what must have been a duck feather stuck in its brim. Dusting it off, he smiled when it fit perfectly. A familiar feeling crept over him, but one he'd never noticed before *away* from home. That was it — he felt... home.

Stepping into an October sun that warmed him briefly, he surveyed his new find. With at least a day's walk to his truck, he grinned with anticipation at the coming night in "his" new cabin. But having forgotten about ducks in the spell of his hidden treasure, he was suddenly hungry. A duck dinner would be a fitting end to such a grand day, he mused. Snugging the brim of the old hat lower, he set off for the end of the point.

The remaining two hours of daylight offered plenty of time. Normally, such a remote pond would be used mid-morning to early afternoon as a place for ducks and maybe a few geese to loaf the day away. But the strip of wild rice was almost as exciting as the cabin, for that meant duck food and, hopefully, some action. Growing up, he'd hunted a place managed for ducks — flooded corn, to be specific. It was like clockwork when those birds would ring the dinner bell. The first and last hours of the day were the best, with not much of anything in between.

While similar feed lakes littered the Upper Peninsula, they usually attracted the attention of duck hunters as well. Scanning the lake with a small pair of binoculars, he was pleased to see no blinds or flipped-over canoes along the shore. Other than Sam's cabin, he doubted anyone had been here before, especially to hunt.

Such places were magnets for certain species in particular. Wood ducks and mallards, of course, along with ringnecks, and maybe a few bluebills mixed in. He never shot a ringneck, but shot *at* a few of those speed demons; maybe this was the day. Regardless of what flew over, he knew wild rice meant above-average tasting meat, on both divers and puddlers, though truth be told, since devouring his last sandwich at noon, he'd happily take a couple of mergansers.

With all that had happened the last two days, it was strange to stand at the point from the cabin and finally go hunting. But first he had to deal with the decoys, namely how to retrieve them once thrown from shore. That water looked mighty black and deep, at least over his hip boots. Luckily, one decoy carried a twelve-foot anchor cord, which he could use to lasso the lines of the others at pickup time, provided they weren't too far away. Six blocks surely wouldn't do the job, but they were all he had, so he'd have to make them come to life.

By running a line under a heavy, submerged log, he was able to fashion a simple jerk string. His dad loved a good jerk cord for motion. "Ducks aren't sedentary," he'd say. But Dad was also old-fashioned and didn't like anything that ran on batteries. "I go to the marsh to get away from the noise, not to bring it with me." And he could relate. He was a lot like that, too, and so far, seclusion was his favorite part about this little paradise.

With enough bog grass to hunker down in and a setup as good as he could make, the waiting game commenced. He'd be an old man and still remember the welcome sound of those fighter-jet ringnecks as they dive-bombed his lake not ten minutes later. Once, twice, three times they circled at what seemed a hundred miles per hour. Wishing to conserve his precious shells, he held his fire even though on two of the passes, the dozen birds were well in range. On the fourth flyby, his impatience — and hunger — got the best of him. He knew it was wrong to flock shoot. Dad would have scolded him, or at least laughed. Not only was it a bum sporting way to get a bird, but highly ineffective.

Pick one bird and stick with it, he told himself, but at the fateful moment, he fired, then again, at all of them and none of them. His heart sank when nothing fell from the departing flock, until a single drake slanted hard seventy-five yards away in the marsh. Never had he wanted a duck so badly, and he galloped to it faster than a retriever. His first ringneck — which should be called "ringbill," he thought, marveling at the white rings around the base and tip of the bill.

Proudly hustling back to his weedy blind, careful not to ruffle the bird's feathers, he wondered if the day could get any better. It did. After saluting two more flocks of divers with nothing to show but the fine smell of spent duck loads, a pair of mallards glided down nearly on top of him. A few mediocre quacks from his call and a handful of tugs on the cord worked like magic, and one of the birds fell on the second shot. Too close to the end of legal shooting light to tell the male from the female, he wasn't being picky. The hen splashed down in six inches of grassy water not far away, and he had a pending meal fit for a king.

Practically giddy, he hauled his six decoys and two prized ducks back to the cabin in the glowing sunset. Thankfully, it didn't look like rain; the hole in the roof and window were obvious leaks, but surely there were others.

Setting his load down near the door, he took a quick but careful stroll around the cabin. Creeping along in the semi-dark, the dwelling seemed more structurally sound than he thought. A couple of old trails led in different directions, maybe walking trails, or to a cache where

The Trapper's Cabin

Sam had kept food safe from the critters. Would his good fortune lead him to a boat?

His thoughts stumbled as much as his feet, and he eventually tripped over the grave. With a lump in his throat, he froze. *Sam?* Not possible. Besides, it was too short. *A child, perhaps?* Maybe, but then his flashlight caught the glint of a buckle from a dog's collar. It was Sam's dog, of course. The bowl in the cabin had belonged to the dog.

Kneeling down, almost reverently, he inspected the gravesite and then the small driftwood cross, still tied together with twine, where the collar hung. Burned into the horizontal piece were two words: *Thanks, Buck.*

A wave of emotions washed over him. With no one around, he didn't wipe away the few tears that trickled down his cheeks; rather, he just knelt there, sad and confused. He'd never met this person before, nor the dog, yet he felt connected. Tears flowed more freely when he remembered his family dog growing up, Jess, an English setter, and how Mom told him it was natural to cry, especially for bird dogs at the end of their hunt.

With enough secrets to unravel, the adventurous part of him that found this place roared back to life, and his wet eyes sparkled at the thought of dinner, the coming night, a roaring fire in the cabin with a hole in its roof, and tomorrow.

Entering through the front door, he paused, placed the ducks on the table, and inhaled deeply through his nose. He *was* home.

—*Chris Smith*

The Gift that Keeps on Giving

Christmas Eve found our extended family gathered around the dining-room table for a traditional holiday supper. As a politically diverse group, we avoid discussing world affairs and upcoming elections, which opens the floor to other topics. While the scalloped potatoes were making a second orbit, someone posed the question: "What was your favorite childhood Christmas gift?"

At first, silence filled the room, but eventually my younger brother kicked the ball into motion, reliving his joy as he unwrapped a Millennium Falcon toy during the height of the original *Star Wars* craze. Inspired by his exuberance, my kids rehashed a more recent Christmas morning when Santa brought scooters, turning our main floor into an impromptu skatepark.

Next came my turn. The question *seemed* simple enough. *A Christmas Story* had been playing nonstop the last few days, so the boy-gets-BB-gun plotline was fresh in my mind. I began flipping through a mental Rolodex of gifted rifles and shotguns. Like Ralphie, an iconic

Daisy Red Ryder had come first, followed by a battery of others. But which qualified as *the* one?

Taking a contemplative sip of pinot noir, my mind drifted back to the 1980s. Reagan was president; the space program was in full swing; and movies like *Red Dawn*, *Back to the Future*, and *Karate Kid* were playing in theaters. In short, it was a fine time to grow up in middle-class America... except for the fact that my liberal-minded parents and I didn't see eye-to-eye about guns.

Then again, who could blame them? By the time I was born, they'd only recently retired their bell-bottoms and Birkenstocks. With world views formed upon a college campus in the late '60s, firearms simply went against their flower-power ethos. Nixon-era politics, war in Southeast Asia, and domestic tragedies like Kent State had made them eternally gunshy.

My brother and I, on the other hand, were weaned on episodes of *Grizzly Adams* and *Gunsmoke*, so revolvers and lever rifles seemed like standard issue. But Mom and Dad refused to budge. No child of theirs would own even a cap pistol, never mind what the neighbor kids were doing. A little imagination went a long way in those pre-social media days, however. We secretly fashioned Lugers out of fallen sticks and bolt rifles from old broom handles.

The lingering hippie spirit within my parents' souls must have breathed a sigh of relief when my brother turned his attention to the wholesome sport of baseball, but I refused to lay down my weapons. Like Luke Skywalker in *The Empire Strikes Back*, I'd sooner cast myself into the abyss than turn to the dark side. I wanted a gun even more than my parents wanted me *not* to have one — which was saying an awful lot. After constant begging and pleading, they finally realized they'd lost the war — an ironic concept for these conscientious objectors.

That Christmas, a long, slender box lay beneath the tree. That first Daisy may have offered a quick and easy answer to the "favorite Christmas gift" question, but it wasn't representative of the broader truth. Doubtless, that spring-action air rifle ferried me over the mountains and into metaphorical Indian Country, but looking back, my experiences outdoors superseded any tangible present. Exploring the outdoors was a gift that would keep on giving long after the Red Ryder had rusted away.

My outdoor journey really began back in 1984, when my closest chum was Tim. We'd been friends since toddlerhood, and aside from the vacant field behind his house, our favorite place on earth was his Uncle Tom and Aunt Mindy's 200-acre farm. There we learned the finer points of marksmanship, stalking, survival, and subsistence hunting.

Tim's aunt and uncle lived close to the soil and looked part American Gothic and part Lynyrd Skynyrd — "salt-of-the-earth" people, as folks say in the Midwest. Mindy was sturdy and independent and equally comfortable splitting wood, playing guitar, or slinging hay bales. She had a gentle heart and a quick smile but never hesitated to gun down a barn rat with the rusty revolver she kept tucked in her belt.

Uncle Tom could have been kin to hairy Esau of Old Testament fame. A reddish thatch of beard covered his ruddy cheeks, and he dressed in threadbare flannel shirts, frayed overalls, and worn leather work boots. Unlike Tim and me, Uncle Tom was strangely immune to biting flies, mosquitoes, and poison ivy. What's more, he earned his living as a professional trapper, patrolling Allegan County's lowlands in an era when quality pelts commanded a princely sum. Legend had it that he could center a deerfly between the eyes with a wad of Red Man chewing tobacco.

Tom and Mindy's whitewashed farmhouse bordered several rusty-red pig barns. Wind and sunlight had weathered their wooden exteriors so severely that they looked like molting iguana skin, and stench of all those jostling swine blanketed the countryside for miles around, lending a signature aroma to the area. Even today, a hint of pig manure on the wind never fails to conjure memories of that place.

Beyond the farmyard, corn and soybean fields stretched to the horizon, terminating at a distant tree line where Potawatomi Indians had camped centuries before. Their flint arrowheads, spear points, and drill bits rose to the surface after spring rains softened the soil.

A distant tree line, barely visible from the farmhouse, formed a transition between agriculture and a wilderness where wood ducks nested among sycamores and the coffee-colored Rabbit River gurgled amid swamp maples. Down there, the night air reverberated with the music of coyotes and great-horned owls.

None of that sprawling countryside or the adjoining fields was public land, but it might as well have been. Property lines meant nothing, and we trespassed with impunity. A couple of wandering kids warranted no cause for concern, and besides, what harm could they do anyway?

As a self-professed "pistol-packing Presbyterian," Mindy frequently quoted verses from the Good Book. Psalm 46 says, "Be still, and know that I am God." We took everything Aunt Mindy said literally, lying motionless for hours along the riverbank, developing the monk-like patience required for successful hunting — and fostering quiet hearts as well.

In autumn and winter, that hinterland was a hunter's paradise, but whenever the mercury topped sixty degrees, mosquitoes and deerflies descended in Biblical plagues. But discomfort was the price of doing business, and our parents allowed us to discover it on our own from an early age. Thanks to their liberal views on supervision, we earned an advanced degree in outdoor education through trial and error — lessons carried into adulthood.

We rolled canoes in the nearly frozen river, fell out of tree stands, crashed through skim ice, and contracted cases of poison ivy so severe we *wished* they were fatal. Our first campfire-cooked wild game was an utter fiasco — ruffed grouse charred on the outside and raw on the inside. Never mind intestinal worms, we were living off the land by our wits, and no disaster ever tasted so satisfying. Before learning how to build a proper shelter and fire reflector, we spent countless nights shivering beneath winter skies, alternately freezing and smoking ourselves like human beef jerky.

What neglectful parents would have allowed this? Didn't someone with a conscience call Child Protective Services? Fortunately not. That freedom to explore, to succeed — and yes, even to fail — was *the ultimate present*, the gift that kept on giving.

It's no secret that society takes food for granted, and a vast majority of the population has no idea what an empty stomach feels like. Tim and I didn't either, until we challenged ourselves to a week in the woods with no food. Our plan was to eat only what we foraged or shot. After days of meager rations, hunger began consuming our thoughts. One morning, in the midst of a ketosis haze, I set out alone, armed only with an 870 Express and a pocketful of sixes. A few hours later, I strode back into camp, game bag bulging with a grouse (my first), rabbit, and two squirrels. Meat filled our bellies, but pride swelled our chests to button-popping proportions.

On inky-black nights when haunting sounds resonated through the timber, we faced down the demons that lurked beyond the firelight. At first, the unknown commotion rattled our nerves and shook our resolve, but eventually we learned a simple truth that remained with us through adulthood: Fear is a mental contrivance that must be overcome.

Outdoor writer Gene Hill once wrote, "Our greatest trophies are not things, but times." Somehow, my non-hunting parents knew that, too, realizing experiences and hard-won independence would supersede any box beneath the Christmas tree. The best present they bestowed was the freedom to spend a childhood outdoors. Guns provided a catalyst, but where they took us was priceless. Then again, the greatest gifts always are.

—Jon Osborn

Backcountry

I think this might be our best chance," I said. We'd tried twice before to load the canoes, but each time, the rain intensified, forcing us to relocate gear and selves back into the Dodge.

"Hold on, I have all four aces. This won't take long," Pete said.

It hadn't for me. Eliminated after three rounds of three-handed War in the car, I turned to jotting thoughts in a camp journal and watching the fat splats of rain on the windshield, trying to judge if they were getting smaller or, at the very least, slowing down. Seven hours and forty-five minutes from home… on the extreme western edge of Michigan's Upper Peninsula… our gear crammed into the back of the SUV to stay as dry as possible for as long as possible… a who-knew-how-long canoe trip to our remote campsite… I suppose there was no rush. No timetable to keep except for the anxiousness of simply striking out and getting gone.

My sons continued. Mark, 14, reclaimed two aces from Pete, 17, in some impressive wars stretching across the car's middle console. I finally flexed parental authority when the rain appeared to slacken as much as it was going to, and they packed away their stacks in a temporary cease-fire to resume in the tent. Which, judging by a final look at the radar, they'd have ample time for. A last call to home complete, and we dashed back down to the boat launch in the light drizzle for that charmed third time.

Since we had a not-so-dry run twice already, it didn't take long to re-nestle our gear into the pair of canoes — a twenty-footer for the boys and a fourteen-foot Kevlar for me. Waves lapped onto the hulls while we stood on the shore gazing out into the lake, the boys with looks of equal parts excitement and terror, me certain I'd lost Parent of the Year by directing my sons out into such a mess. As if to make my point, the rain picked up and a gust bent the oaks and pines over a channel on the other end of the lake — which, for now, was simply a sheltered portion of the 565-acre, spidery-shaped Crooked Lake.

"Okay, listen up, boys," I said in my best ship captain's voice, trying to hide the tremor. "Life jackets at all times. We stick close to shore in case we need to head for cover. Any thunder or lightning, don't wait for me, just get to land. If you tip, don't worry about the gear; kick free and get to shore. Work together. And don't race up ahead — wait for me. I'm old."

Receiving a verbal, "Got it" from both, I shoved them off — Pete in the stern, Mark in the bow, and a mound of gear between them. Both boys are experienced in the outdoors, of course, but they're also cadet members of the Civil Air Patrol. This U.S. Air Force Auxiliary formed in 1941 so private citizen aircraft owners could use their own planes to monitor the coastlines for any German or Japanese soldiers hitting our shores when things heated up overseas. Passionate for aviation, Pete joined a few years prior in anticipation of applying to the Air Force Academy, a longing that had recently changed to emergency medicine as a nurse on a chopper where, as he put it, "they won't be shooting at me." Not long after Pete started, Mark followed in his big brother's footsteps and joined to spend time together and to fuel his enthusiasm for engineering.

After the war, the main thrust of CAP's charter became one of search-and-rescue and field first aid for anything involving lost hikers, downed planes, or natural disasters. The first aerial photos taken over the smoking piles of Towers One and Two were taken by a CAP plane. As part of search-and-rescue training, CAP members learn a bit about wilderness living, for when they're on a search mission, ground teams pretty much sleep where they are. It was this aspect of their training that the boys wanted to stretch outside of a simulated scenario. I hoped we wouldn't need the first aid and rescue parts.

In truth, they were more qualified to take care of me than I was of them.

I wedged myself in the back of my canoe and followed in their wake.

The drive across the Upper Peninsula the day before had been wonderfully mundane for mid-August. The familiar bastion of wilderness basked in the summer sunshine, endless waves of green grass and trees pulsating in a perpetual wind. The boys were at the perfect age for a backcountry experience — a time to get away, just the three of us, some brotherly bonding, Mark at 14 old enough and responsible enough to carry his weight, Pete at 17 thinking those big thoughts as high school neared its end. As a parent, your main job is to keep kids safe, something I already failed at by shoving them off in their own canoe into the powerful and indiscriminate wilderness. Next is to make sure that siblings stay friends. Pete and Mark get along very well, but it's always nice to have opportunities to grow together, especially in such a remote location, where we depend on our wits and one another.

They were also at the right age to learn that there was something… *more*. Teenage boys — even those not wrapped up in social media, which, thankfully my guys are not — can have a Ptolemaic view of the world. Right after safety and sibling relationships, a parent's job is to teach them not everything revolves around them, that things can rise up and squash them without losing a wink of sleep. And that no matter your position in the batting lineup or the drumline or your grades or your Instagram audience or clever tweets you can conjure, time will go on ticking just the same.

The Sylvania Wilderness Area provided the perfect setting. Lying within the Ottawa National Forest, Sylvania is what we refer to as a "mini Boundary Waters." Not quite as remote, not quite as rich of a fishery, but fantastic tradeoffs for being not quite as popular and not quite as far from home. Thirty-six unique lakes and nineteen ponds are connected through a series of portages ranging from a quick stroll, to the Oregon Trail without the wagons but perhaps the dysentery. It takes some effort to secure a rustic campsite earlier in the year, but after some trial and error, we found two next to each other in a secluded cove on Crooked Lake, one of the two main lakes campers and canoers set out from. I grabbed them both to block an interloper from setting up shop next to us and ruining the bit of wilderness we craved.

Upon entering the park and registering, you're required to watch a "leave no trace" type video before setting out. I asked about mountain lion sightings, which I'd noticed in a report while reserving the campsites.

"Oh, they're around, we've found tracks," the ranger, a high schooler manning the desk for the summer, had said. She glanced sideways at Pete. "But we haven't seen any. They shouldn't bother you."

"Bears?" I asked. Mark's eyes widened.

"For sure," she said. "But if your food's in a tree, you'll be fine."

It wasn't just the wilderness that didn't really care about you or what you did back home. Neither did the locals.

But it was still part of our world, and a part the boys needed to experience. And yet, knowing what they knew about how to take care of themselves — even if unexperienced at putting their knowledge into action — a parental nerve tremored deep down. I realized we struck out from shore more as teammates and colleagues instead of coach and players, teacher and students. Perhaps Sylvania had something to teach me, too. Watching my sons row out into the beautifully grim, silver, smudgy lake, a kaleidoscope of grays roiling across the treetops, I happened to learn the lesson at the beginning of the trip instead of the end. That to move on with anything, there comes a moment of letting go to what held you or bound you or grounded you, and trusting in whatever you've crammed into your brain and forging ahead. And my "letting go" paddled ahead of me into the gloom, out of my control.

I didn't like it.

We stopped momentarily in the channel connecting the sheltered portion around the boat launch to the main belly of the wide — and potentially tumultuous — Crooked Lake. I reminded the boys to stay close to shore.

A moderate chop greeted us — thankfully not the whitecaps near the shore I expected — but the rain and wind pounded us straight in the face. I quickly stashed my worthless glasses and surrendered to the drenching. And when I did, I realized it wasn't that cold and that progress was best made one paddle at a time. The heavy canoe held straight and knifed through the rollers, and the far shore and channel connecting to the next finger of the sprawling lake drew closer.

The boys battled, though — not with each other, but against the elements. Ptolemy would've been proud. They wanted to subdue the wind and the rain, bend its will to theirs, and paddle where and how they wanted. Little did they know the wind had been angling their bow ever so slightly to the middle and depths of the lake where the wave tops crumbled under the wind into a spray of white. A confusion of which side to paddle on — and combined with the arm strength of a 14-year-old in the bow compared to a 17-year-old in the stern — led to the canoe turning broadside in the waves.

I whistled above the wind — a sharp, piercing, single blast with fingers curled to my lips. My dad whistled like that. He could stop me in my tracks with it on the basketball court amid cheering fans to give me shooting pointers from the stands. I motioned for them to work toward me, closer to shore, and they fell into sync.

"Calm down. One stroke at a time. You're already wet, so there's no rush to get to the campsite. You can't get 'more wet' unless you tip, so work together and keep it straight."

Maybe the Old Man could still teach them something. They couldn't bend the wilderness to them; they had to become part of it and glide their way through it. And in seconds — and hugging close to shore — they stretched out a lead ahead of me.

At the far end of the widest and longest section, the waves calmed, and we pulled into another channel, the wind duking it out with the treetops. A lone loon sat in the middle of the channel, and we paddled on either side of him, not more than ten yards away. He showed little urge to do anything other than simply sit in the rain. The twisty channel drew us deeper into the backcountry, depositing us into an open straightaway lined on either side by towering wild rice, and then we crossed into the last long section of Crooked Lake. No other campers showed themselves in the slop, and using the mental satellite image from the last look at the map back in the car, I turned us into our cove, our campsites at the far end.

We beached. We had fought and battled and wrestled with — and ultimately vanquished — a bit of Nature.

The trees bent, the rain unleashed, and a mass of ugly clouds darkened the sky.

Nature didn't care. It didn't even know we were there.

No time to enjoy our surroundings. The boys' Civil Air Patrol training kicked in. Out came the tarps and paracord; a few lashes around gnarly old cedars, and they fashioned a makeshift lean-to, a tarp on the ground, gear and firewood stashed underneath to begin the drying process. We picked the more level and spacious of the two campsites, quickly set the tent, and dashed inside to begin *our* drying process, which involved a change of clothes for each of us.

"Take off your socks and dry your feet," Pete recommended as we sprawled out the sleeping bags and pillows — dry from their boat ride in thick, contractor garbage bags. "That's what they taught us at PJOC." PJOC — Air Force Pararescue and Survival Orientation Course — is a Civil Air Patrol extracurricular camp in the New Mexico wilderness run by Air Force Special Forces. Pete trained months for it and attended the summer before our trip; but a dislocated kneecap — something he'd suffered during a successful summit of Half Dome in Yosemite the year before, another loss for Parent of the Year — almost prevented him from attending. After having to pass a physical test of push-ups, sit-ups, pull-ups, and distance running in order to even board the bus at Kirtland Air Force Base to head into the mountains, the jinky kneecap prompted a call home while the bus idled, waiting for him. Luckily, the CAP colonel talked to my wife Vickie — the one who joined him on the Half Dome trek, though she didn't summit — and not me.

"What do you *want* to do?" she had asked him on the phone. Pete, in tears because of the pain, didn't want to be a burden to his teammates if he were injured. "You trained a long time for this!"

"I want to get on the bus," he finally said.

"*Then get on the bus!*" she ordered like a commanding officer. He popped his kneecap back into place, said, "Love you Mom," boarded the bus, and graduated the survival course.

He didn't know at the time that she broke down afterward, thinking she'd just sent her son to his doom.

PJOC marked the turning point in Pete's desire for the military, a desire that scared me to my core ever since he started talking about it at 13 years old. Listening to the Air Force personnel talk about their jobs was exciting, but they also pointed out how much their families hated it and how much it took away from their time at home — a deal-breaker for Pete. I told him afterward that the camp proved some of the best money we ever spent, for it helped direct his path even if in a direction he hadn't expected. "Better to find out now instead of two weeks into boot camp," I said.

In the tent in dry clothes and bare feet two hours after shoving off from the paved boat launch, the game of War resumed. Pete eventually vanquished Mark. I stretched out and listened, gauging the storm's passing by the diminishing of the sound of rain pelting the tent and the forest's growing silence.

We finally took a survey. I tossed more paracord around a high tree branch, and Mark wrapped the tag end around a stump for a handle; together, we pullied the cooler high off the ground to prevent curious bears from figuring out the menu. The boys scavenged bits of firewood and kindling from the sister campsite and surrounding forest — pretty picked over — while I walked up a short rise inland and located the pit toilet. No way either of them would use it except in an absolute gastric emergency; it wasn't too high on my list, either. I chanced a peek at civilization and noticed one bar on my cellphone, dashed off a text to my wife, and told her I would try again in the evening.

That's when I noticed that, in the hullabaloo of the rain and setting the tent and stowing the gear, we'd placed our tent in a most unfortunate place. A towering oak, for whatever reason, had grown out from the side of the short rise toward the lake before curving upward, like a leaning palm tree stretching from the jungle to the ocean on a postcard-perfect Caribbean beach. And our tent sat right under it. It swayed in the remnant wind from the storm.

"Deadman's Camp," I muttered. Perfect. The boys got a laugh out of it. I made sure the tree wasn't rotting.

We hoped to get in some fishing on the trip, although mid-August isn't the best time to fill up on panfish from the chain of lakes in Sylvania. A lead from returning campers earlier in the day pointed us to one lake off the beaten path for catch-and-release smallmouth bass. While we busied about like the mosquitoes finding fresh meat, we made a plan to hit Loon Lake the next day for a real fishing trip.

"We'll pack lunches for the boat, leave mid-morning, make a day of it," I said, arranging the water cooler, camp pans, and pots, hoping for at least one of them to wrangle with a bass. We dropped the dry, gas-station firewood near the fire ring. "For now, let's take a boat ride on Crooked Lake for a look around." Neither kid appeared too thrilled about getting back into the boat after the adventure out, but I played the Dad card. It didn't work in War, but it did here.

Crooked Lake was turbid, but the boys got a sense of its enormity, missed during the drenching affair from hours earlier and the singular focus of finding the cove and shelter. The world seemed to be shaking off the rain as if fluffing its feathers. An eagle soared overhead. We saw more loons. The sun glittered on the surface. The eerie absence of the white noise of daily sounds, like the entire world lost electricity, consumed us; and I think it began to set in on Pete and Mark that, at least for the next few days, the world boiled down to the three of us.

And many other things that held a vote, too. Mark described an encounter best in the camp journal, paraphrasing the schtick of an NPR comedian whose name escapes me:

We decided around 5:30-ish to go fishing, where a conversation like this happened:

Pete: Oh look! A turtle.

Dad: No... is that a sea otter? [To be fair, I meant "river otter."]

Pete: It can't be.

Dad: Well, then it's a log.

Pete: It is NOT a log.

Dad:

Pete:

Me:

Dad: Then that's a snapping turtle! Go! Backward! BACKWARD!

Have you ever heard the sound of screeching tires on water? I have.

I consider myself a fairly decent conservationist, interested in the welfare of all wildlife and a firm supporter of the tool of hunting and other methods for proven and effective wildlife management. But snapping turtles stir a prehistoric fear in me that's embedded in my DNA. If they moved as fast as the movie-version velociraptor, I'm certain they would've taken over the planet, extinction-level-event asteroids be damned. I won't go so far as to say they deserve a place in the Underworld alongside mosquitoes, clingy clear plastic food wrap, and pretty much all social media platforms, but maybe Purgatory.

Food occupies a good deal of the mind when camping, and most certainly for two teenage boys and a middle-aged dad who doesn't need to answer to the scale for a few days. To that end, I'd taken more care of the menu leading up to the trip than whether or not we carried enough paracord or remembered the entrenching tool. And I wanted preparing the food to become some life skill woodsmanship for Pete and Mark. Not that I figured they'd need it in the event of a zombie apocalypse or anything, but it's good to know. And kind of fun. And it had to be more than simply hot dogs. Freezing all the food made them into makeshift ice blocks to keep everything else cool while they gradually thawed, and Pete pried out the hamburger patties, seasoned them up, and set them on the fire grate over the snapping flames. I dumped half of a bag of frozen French fries into a skillet of oil over a propane heater, and Mark busied about the site preparing plates and drinks and paper towels. We took our time, allowing the meal preparation to eat away at the evening, the firelight licking at the softening sky and approaching night. By the time we finished hearty cheeseburgers and fries, we couldn't cram a single s'more in.

While they tended the fire, I returned to the spot of one bar on the cellphone and powered up. The battery had drained substantially, so I didn't know how much juice remained for the trip. A text from Vickie sat waiting:

A WHAT?!?!? Are you guys all right?!?!?

"What is she talking about?" I mumbled. I scrolled up to my text from earlier in the afternoon: *We're at the campsite. Already saw one lion. Boys did great. Will try again tonight.*

"Oh. Whoops. That's an unfortunate autocorrect."

The good and gracious Lord smiled down on me and briefly added another bar on the cellphone network.

LOL. Loon, not lion. Sorry about that. Losing battery already. We're fine. Beautifully quiet here.

In the history of husband apologies, it wasn't the best.

I can never sleep past the first hint of dawn while camping, which is fine with me because I love that time of day. Listening to the world greet a new morning, watching the sides of the tent lighten as if on a dimmer switch, grabbing a long-sleeved shirt for a welcome chill on a mid-August morning... it's a precious few moments when everything stretches and yawns and is unaware and sort of rests in its place in the world. Vulnerable but not helpless. Just alive.

Being teenage boys and zonked out, Pete and Mark didn't notice any of this, allowing me some morning quiet while setting the pot for coffee on the propane heater. Since we'd be shoving off soon, I didn't want to start a fire and chance leaving it hot and smoking and unattended. Coffee in hand in a tin cup, I leaned up against a tree on the shoreline — vulnerable, alive — and watched the calm water transform into purple and silver in the waxing light.

These morning rituals take on new meaning when you're alone in the wilderness, especially if others depend on you. Heat. Nourishment. Shelter. Yes, all of this occurred on a greatly minimized scale compared to actually being lost in the wilderness after surviving a plane crash in the Alaskan bush, staying alive on our wits and what we could scavenge. I mean, we brought French fries after all. And right now, in a cooler hoisted into a tree, three thick steaks sat thawing that, apparently, the bears didn't find appetizing. There's a great deal of calm that follows doing something like this on purpose compared to when it's unexpected.

But for the world around us and everything in it, this could've been the Alaskan bush. It was their daily survival and fight for it that we inserted ourselves into for no other reason than to simply be a part of it. Not to overpower or overcome, but to witness. To coexist in a place where the birds and the snapping turtles and the otters and the bears and the trees were the experts. And French fries or not, one tip of the canoe on the fishing trip ahead or an errant miscalculation with a knife we all carried, and suddenly the "on purpose" would, indeed, become "unexpected."

Vulnerable. Alive.

I reminded the boys of that as we downed the last English muffin egg sandwich around the skillet on the propane and they grumbled a bit about life jackets. We reviewed the lake maps, found our portage first from Crooked Lake to Clark Lake and then from Clark to Loon, triple-checked the gear we wanted to take, and piled into the three-seat, twenty-foot canoe.

A couple of fishing boats sat scattered across Crooked Lake. Motors are allowed on Crooked, for it has public access, but not on the connecting lakes, accessible only through the portages. Our first up-and-down portage brought us out to a sandy beach on Clark, the other entry lake in the Sylvania system. There, whitecaps rolled in the middle of the windswept lake, and clear, deep water along shore promised a spot for a rustic "bath" should the need arise.

We found the narrow steps and trail for the next portage. Mark and I tried to figure out how best to tandem carry the canoe; but Pete pushed us aside, asked me how a single person carries a canoe with the built-in yoke, and, after I showed him, lifted it onto his shoulders and struck off.

"Okay, then," Mark said, watching his older brother scamper into the woods. We saddled the fishing tackle and lunches in his wake, thankful we weren't hauling all of our camping and cooking gear on the trek to one of Loon Lake's few campsites.

Coming out onto Loon Lake felt as if we'd found an undiscovered jewel. While Crooked Lake held no homes past the boat launch, there still appeared evidence of people. Beaten down trails visible from the water, smoke chimneying through the cedars, boats pulled up onto shore. Loon Lake sat utterly empty. We could've been in the Northwest Territories or Alaska or Belize, if Belize had cedars and smallmouth bass and not mangroves and creatures that wanted to eat you or poison you for the fun of it. This was sheer abandonment of society, left behind by "progress" to its own fate, a forgotten dimple on the world. And it made me reconsider hauling the camping and cooking gear on the tortuous portage the next time we visited.

Less than a hundred yards from the entry point, I hit the first smallmouth on a green rubber worm. The bass were everywhere. And hungry in the bright, late morning. Along shore in the shadows, on the sandy drop-off we saw clearly twenty feet below through the magically turquoise water, either side of the boat we casted produced a hook-up. And with the osprey spiraling overhead and loons calling and sunlight sparkling on the water like shattering glass and all manner of wildlife flitting along the shore....

Yeah. We were staying here next time.

Ranging in size from twelve to seventeen inches, the bronzebacks doubled over our light spinning tackle and made me wish we'd remembered a net and attempted to bring a fly rod. Too many fish caught to remember each fight, I am left to the few photos of the boys holding them up, bright grins, an untouched land in the backdrop. The day led to a sentence I'm not sure has ever been uttered by a teenage boy when Mark reeled in, clipped the hook, set the rod down, and leaned back in the middle seat: "I'm tired." From catching fish. He was tired from catching fish. For a glorious stretch, we were "those guys" who articles are written about and TV shows are produced for and big tackle company sponsorships are handed out to. We couldn't do anything wrong.

Except I did leave the bail on the reel open at one point while I paddled. A fish rising more than a hundred yards behind the boat surprised us until we realized it wasn't a rise at all but a smallmouth tangling with the fake worm that had been trailing behind the boat. Longest reel-in of a fish in Smith Family history.

The peanut butter and jelly sandwiches in the boat didn't do the trick, and our own grumbling stomachs finally conquered those of the bass. With a final family timer photo shot — note: *not* a selfie — we bid "until next time" to Loon Lake.

A nap in a quiet forest sounds heavenly, but I can't do it, particularly when it's hot. So I puttered about the camp in the afternoon while the boys lazed away in the tent. The steaks were thawing nicely to cook over the fire; fingerling potatoes would be fried on the propane; and the water from the cooler, pretty much air-temperature, felt refreshing on my face and neck and back. If I were a true woodsman, I wouldn't have bothered and rather embraced the layer of grime as one more step back to a pioneer. But, again, store-bought steaks and propane and tents surrounded me. Only a toe dangled into the true world of the wild.

Still, as the boys roused, I spotted the camp hatchet and hefted it, testing its balance. This could be a valuable skill to learn in the event of a rabid black bear invading the camp. Or a mountain lion. Or a zombie.

"Hey boys," I said, finding a suitably rotten tree abused by the pileated woodpeckers. "I think we should learn how to throw a hatchet."

Their eyes brightened with mischief.

"Well, Mom *isn't* here..." Mark said. Because he'd spent only fourteen years with Vickie, nine of which he probably remembered, and not the twenty-five I had, he didn't know that his mother, had she been there, would be the first up to the line.

It took a few tosses, but we eventually got the hang of the proper wrist flick to send the hatchet tumbling end over end and plunging deep into the rotted maple tree. Contests ensued, winners were crowned, and we deemed ourselves suitably armed to protect the camp if the wild bared its teeth.

The joviality of it all almost stopped immediately, though, when Pete tossed the hatchet from hand to hand. In a blink, the "on purpose" came within a hair's breadth of the "unexpected" when the blade sliced his finger nearly clean to the bone. Almost unnoticeably, he excused himself to the tent where his field first-aid lessons from Civil Air Patrol took over. A few Band-Aids, gauze, and some athletic tape later, he returned.

The perfectly clear sky promised an even better show of stars. Because the potatoes took so long, the steaks got overcooked, but we didn't care. We used our pocketknives like shining flatware at a fancy restaurant. We took slow-motion pictures and videos of the fire as night encroached, Pete poking a stick into the logs to create an eruption of sparks that Mark captured. We grew quiet, our strength draining. We melted into the darkness.

I lost myself in the fire. They amaze me. Fires are as old as anything can be old. For some reason, I've always imagined fire sparking from the fingertips of God Himself in those first six busy days of reality, if mankind can be so arrogant as to attribute its definition of a "day" to that of God's. Fire changed the course of man perhaps more than any other creation, but for all its controlled and contained forms, the barely tamed campfire, licking at an unpolluted night sky, still astounds me.

It is a blindfolded scale of the universe, keeping everything in balance. As something grows, something else diminishes. Not just within the fire itself, but also within those who sit and watch and wonder about their place in things. Especially for those who, at their core, try desperately to keep the embers of a wild spirit smoldering in the midst of an increasingly concrete existence. For within a fire is the very essence of life and death, creation and destruction, desire and sacrifice. It is a small part of yourself that wonders if the encroaching ails of a world gone mad will be kept at bay for a little while, and losing yourself in a quiet peace that tells you, Yes, they will. Therein lies the paradox that fuels a wild spirit.

Pure darkness comes early when that concrete world is miles and miles away. And the stars, always present even beyond the blue sky, revealed themselves. The boys and I stood in awe. The Milky Way dust arced up from the pitch-black horizon line, a faint wash of orange illuminating stars incomprehensible distances away. We tried long-exposure setting photos to show Vickie and Maddie back home, but they didn't do the canvas before us justice — for a great Cosmic Canvas is the only apt description I can find. A canvas for The Painter.

I had company with my coffee the next morning. Strolling by the lakeshore while the boys slept, a mink slithered up onto a log carrying a bluegill. I apologized for disturbing him and told him I like fish for breakfast, too, but I prefer mine on a piece of buttered toast. He oozed back into the water, taking his meal to-go, and popped up down the shore.

A flitting in front brought me up a step. Except for some black-capped chickadees, we'd seen precious few birds around camp. I gave a *psh-psh-psh-psh* call; long ago, a family friend taught it to me as the easiest way to call in all manner of curious songbirds. I'm not sure what they think the noise is — I meant "Good morning" with it — but it certainly intrigues them. A chickadee did come to inspect, and he brought with him a few friends. Apparently, this single cedar tree I stood beneath was a rest area for a warbler migration. I quickly recognized I'd never seen some of these birds before, even after being in the warbler migrations along the Straits of Mackinac in a wonderful summer Vickie and I spent working for the Forest Service. There were so many different ones, I knew I'd never remember my mental photos accurately, so I crept away, dashed back to camp, and grabbed the camera. Returning, a few more *psh-psh-psh* calls brought them back, all in bright adult plumage, all sitting prettily for photos I later keyed out alongside my college bird book — black-throated green, black-and-white, pine, bay-breasted, yellow-rumped, and my favorite the black-throated blue. They hopped from branch to branch, wondering if I were a threat or a provider of food or just another traveler, like them.

The day morphed into something a bit gloomier and chillier than the perfection from our fishing trip — clammy, reminiscent of our initial foray into the backcountry. With no real destination, we decided to explore. We portaged to nearby Mountain Lake and its harrowingly black abyss. In a Crooked Lake cove, we tried to decipher the *tsk-tsk-tsk* chastising us from the shadows of a tangle of blowdowns along the shore. A sleek otter slid into the water and waked down the shore, urging us to follow, stopping to make sure, and then continuing. I knew better and glanced in the opposite direction, and there, using a blowdown for cover, two sets of eyes watched us. I whispered to the guys and pointed with my paddle. Mama otter saw the jig was up, so she darted back to her young, collected them, and in three large circles, they disappeared into the lake.

I felt it close to dinnertime — those first, unmistakable tremors of the "modern" world upon my mind. Plans. The next day, seven hours and forty-five minutes away, the boys had their marching band photos for school at six in the evening. We would cross a time zone in the central U.P. and lose an hour, so breakfast, striking camp, the long canoe ride, and the even longer drive home had to be accounted for. For some reason, the guys wanted to grab a shower before heading down to the football field for what ended up being bleary-eyed photos in their uniforms. Working the clock backward, it pointed to a painful rise and departure time and the necessity for nothing to go wrong.

That clamminess coated the firewood, and the hot dogs took a while to sizzle over nothing more than a pilot-light's flame and a tower of smoke. We packed what we could, left only the tent and duffels to finish in the morning, and hit the rack early.

Nothing did, amazingly, go wrong. The boys managed the ride out much more expertly than on the way in, their brotherliness strengthening into a companionship I hope they nurture their entire lives. Breaching the last archway of trees over the lake channel leading into the bay around the boat launch, they kicked it into high gear, the goal in sight, slicing through the water like true woodsmen, leaving me far behind as I watched them make landfall.

And as I looked behind me at the arch of trees over the lake channel curving off into early morning shadows, I realized I'd left a part of my wild spirit in that backcountry. The country was so big back there, and everything seemed so small before me. Except for the boys on shore, urging me on. And the family waiting for me seven hours and forty-five minutes away. And the life we all shared together.

Driving across the Mackinaw Bridge with the boys completely passed out, the blue of the Straits sprawling into the horizon on either side, I rolled the past few days around in my head. I saw it all again, flickers of highlights culminating in a final timer photo of the three of us at the boat launch. And one of Pete with his arm around Mark, who flashed a thumbs-up, both exhausted yet victorious.

I prayed they learned the lesson. That there is... *more*. That we are but bit players on this wonderful stage, fortunate yet tiny witnesses to the grand passage of time and the elements and the wilderness and the sky and the stars.

And that as witnesses, we might as well enjoy the company of those we have been blessed to live this life with, for however long we are blessed to live it.

—Jake Smith

About the Authors

Greg Frey is an elementary school teacher, fly-fishing guide, and freelance writer. He lives in Petoskey, Michigan. When not guiding on the Jordan, Manistee, Black, and Boyne rivers, he can be found multi-tasking between teaching fourth graders and sixth graders online. It's a lot like wrangling cats without (usually) getting scratched or bitten.

Chris Smith is a wildlife artist and author from Suttons Bay, Michigan, with an incredibly understanding wife, two kids, and two Labs. He's won just enough state duck stamp competitions to justify his hunting and fishing habits as "field research" to his family, though they grew wise a long time ago. Chris believes that God put our eyes next to each other so that we'd shoot side-by-sides, brook trout are the perfect fish regardless of size, and every outing goes better when supervised by a good bird dog.

One of the sobering epiphanies of **Jon Osborn**'s life arrived when he realized that raising teenagers consumes 97.78 percent of a given day. Since then, he resolved to divide any remaining moments among fly fishing, upland hunting, foraging, and writing. Jon, his wife, two kids, and a tri-colored setter live in southwest Michigan, where trout and wild birds exist just far enough away to make every trip afield special.

Jake Smith is the editor of *The Pointing Dog Journal*, *The Retriever Journal*, and *Just Labs* magazines, as well as the author of the family, faith, and baseball novel *Wish*. He lives in Traverse City, Michigan, with his wife, three kids, and three Labradors. You'd think being the editor of three dog magazines that his dogs would be well-trained, but they're knuckleheads.

Made in the USA
Middletown, DE
25 April 2022